Advance pra

"How wonderful that in these pages Jakusho Kwong-roshi shares the wisdom of a lifetime dedicated to Zen practice! This is a Dharma feast for us all to partake of. It seems that the essential Soto Zen practice is analogous to aspects of Mahamudra, pointing to the similarity in the Buddhist approach to understanding the mind. We welcome this clear instruction lighting the way to direct realization of the nature of the mind."
—VEN. TENZIN PALMO

"*Mind Sky* is Jakusho Kwong-roshi at his best! As ever, his teaching is direct and straightforward, full of compassion, wisdom, and gentle humor. He teaches that Zen practice encompasses samadhi and vipassana, but that Zen meditation goes beyond, to a state of 'silent illumination'—shikantaza—just sitting. He emphasizes that realization can come through one's own experience, not only on the meditation cushion but in normal day-to-day life. Kwong-roshi's unique calligraphy in *Mind Sky* expresses a state of mind as vast and clear as the unclouded sky. Congratulations on this new book!"
—DHAMMANANDA BHIKKHUNI [Chatsumarn Kabilsingh]

"Kwong-roshi has been a true friend to my family and to students of Chögyam Trungpa Rinpoche for many years. That he is a deeply realized teacher is evident in his new book, *Mind Sky*. He joins practical instruction in sitting meditation with his profound but effortless understanding of the nature of things as they are. He shows us how to live and practice always in the present moment. I know that countless readers will benefit from this new volume, based on his teachings at Sonoma Mountain Zen Center."
—DRUK SAKYONG WANGMO [Lady Diana, widow of Chögyam Trungpa Rinpoche]

"In *Mind Sky*, Jakusho Kwong-roshi points at practice and realization in our everyday life, and compassionately encourages us in our practice. *Mind Sky* invites us to become deeply intimate with our life and, in the process, embody the profound teachings from our ancient predecessors."
—CHADE-MENG TAN, author of *Search Inside Yourself* and *Joy on Demand*

Jakusho Kwong-roshi

MIND SKY

Zen Teaching on Living and Dying

Text and Calligraphy by **Jakusho Kwong**

Foreword by Shohaku Okumura
Edited by Sally Scoville

Wisdom Publications
199 Elm Street
Somerville, MA 02144 USA
wisdomexperience.org

Page 175 constitutes a continuation of this copyright page.

Library of Congress Cataloging-in-Publication Data
Names: Kwong, Jakusho, author. | Scoville, Sally, editor.
Title: Mind sky: Zen teaching on living and dying / Jakusho Kwong;
    foreword by Shōhaku Okumura; edited by Sally Scoville.
Description: First. | Somerville: Wisdom Publications, 2022.
Identifiers: LCCN 2021034795 (print) | LCCN 2021034796 (ebook) |
    ISBN 9781614297598 (paperback) | ISBN 9781614297789 (ebook)
Subjects: LCSH: Zen Buddhism—Essence, genius, nature. |
    Zen Buddhism—History. | Dōgen, 1200–1253.
Classification: LCC BQ9265.9 .K96 2022 (print) | LCC BQ9265.9 (ebook) |
    DDC 294.3/927—dc23
LC record available at https://lccn.loc.gov/2021034795
LC ebook record available at https://lccn.loc.gov/2021034796

ISBN 978-1-61429-759-8   ebook ISBN 978-1-61429-778-9

26 25 24 23 22   5 4 3 2 1

Calligraphy by Jakusho Kwong. Cover design by Marc Whitaker.
Interior design by Gopa & Ted2, Inc.

Please visit fscus.org.

Dedicated to
Shunryu Suzuki-roshi and Hoitsu Suzuki-roshi
and to the myriad beings who are all on the same journey.

May these unspoken words be useful.

*During zazen, anything that comes in your mind will
eventually leave, because nothing is permanent.
A thought is like a little cloud moving across the blue sky.
Nothing disturbs that all-encompassing vastness.*

CONTENTS

Foreword xiii

Editor's Preface xvii

Author's Preface xxi

Unwinding a Ball of Yarn 1

Emptying into Spaciousness 3

Way-Seeking Mind 13

Just Sitting 19

Levels of Awareness 21

Young Dogen's Resolve 25

Presentness 29

The Texture of Emptiness 35

Water Is Wet 41

Moment to Moment 43

One Unbroken Moment 47

Bussho: The Buddha-Nature 51

Uji: The Quick of Time 59

Katto: Intertwining Vines   65

Ten Thousand Ripples   69

Sitting in the Dark   73

Fear   77

Sonoma Mountain Koan   79

Suffering and Pain   83

Form and Reflection   87

Zen Stitching   89

Jukai   93

Shiho: Transmission Ceremony   95

The Spirit of Practice   101

The Nature of Ritual   105

Touching the Water   109

Paul Discoe's Teahouse and Wabi-Sabi   113

Dying with Living   117

Bodhidharma's Transmission   119

The One Great Matter   123

A True Friend   127

The Korean Mala: On Dana   131

Past Time Becomes Present:
Chögyam Trungpa Rinpoche   135

Dying Well   143

Remembering Mitsu Suzuki   147

Sekito's Hermitage   155

The Great Fire on Sonoma Mountain   165

APPENDIXES   169

    Nagarjuna's Twelve Links of
    Dependent Origination   170

    Unshu Instruction   173

Credits   175

About the Author   177

FOREWORD

THE TITLE OF Jakusho Kwong's book, *Mind Sky*, reminds me of an expression of the Chinese Zen master Sekito: "The vast sky does not obstruct white clouds floating freely."

Jakusho Kwong tells us that one of the Buddha's universal precepts is clarifying the mind, clearing it of obstructions—that is, all the distracting, dualistic, delusive thinking of our troubled everyday lives. The purpose of Zen meditation—*zazen*—is just this: to clarify the mind. And we can do this not only in seated meditation but all the time in our ordinary lives.

This is an extraordinary period for the entire human world. The years 2020 and 2021 brought the COVID-19 pandemic. We have many natural disasters around the world, such as typhoons, hurricanes, forest fires, locust plagues, drought. Not only are there these difficulties caused by nature, but we also have the many human problems that cause separation between people and between nations. Although this is really a difficult, sad, and painful time, it is also an opportunity to reflect on how we can best live in modern society and to try to find out how we can live harmoniously with all beings in nature. We see separation—but also interconnection. We need to work with all the natural disasters, but we also need to work on inner obstacles caused by the human self-centered mind. To do so, we need to discover the Mind Sky that includes everything and supports everything without discrimination. In this book, Kwong-roshi gives Dharma discourses on various important points in Zen practice itself. He frequently emphasizes the importance of understanding impermanence, which the title refers to, and of transcending dualistic thinking, seeing everything without discrimination.

A bit of history: In 1972, when I began to practice at Antai-ji with Uchiyama-roshi, he asked me to study English. Many Westerners came there to practice with him, and Uchiyama-roshi thought there should be some Japanese practitioners with a clear understanding of the Buddha's and Dogen Zenji's teachings, and thorough experience of zazen practice, who would be able to express the Dharma in English for the future development of Zen Buddhism outside Japan. He sent me and two other disciples to an English school in Osaka that was run by one of Shunryu Suzuki-roshi's disciples. Until then, I had not been at all interested in learning English, but somehow I could not say no to my teacher. I studied English there for three years. In this way I began to feel a strong connection to Suzuki-roshi—and, subsequently, I connected with one of his first students, Jakusho Kwong.

I first met Jakusho Kwong-roshi when he visited Kyoto in 1984, when I was teaching at Kyoto Soto Zen Center. My wife, Yuko, and I met him at the train station and took him to visit Uchiyama-roshi, who lived in Noke-in temple in Kohata, Uji. My immediate impression of Jakusho was that he was a very gentle person with a great sense of humor. When he was talking with Uchiyama-roshi and his wife, he was always smiling.

I first visited Kwong-roshi at Sonoma Mountain Zen Center in 1988, when I was sent by Sotoshu Shumucho to the United States to visit several Zen centers and give Dharma talks. I was impressed by the beauty of nature at Sonoma Mountain Zen Center, with its giant oak trees and redwood forest. Kwong-roshi told me about how he and his sangha had worked from scratch to create a Zen temple—Genjo-ji. An old barn was renovated to become the zendo. I enjoyed sitting there in the zendo, next to the huge Avalokiteshvara statue. Since then I have visited Genjo-ji

Jakusho Kwong (second from left) visiting Kosho Uchiyama (far left)
in Japan with Shohaku Okumura and his wife

several times. During each visit I have appreciated the warm atmosphere of the Zen Center, and the ease and hospitality of Kwong-roshi and his wife, Shinko, along with his sangha.

One time, when I was staying in the cabin near the bathhouse, I was surprised to see a flock of wild turkeys come down from the hill and walk toward my cabin at around five o'clock in the afternoon. Some of them flew up to the high branches of the trees and others onto the roof of the cabin. They came again around the same time the next day. They were so at home, and behaved so naturally, without any caution toward human beings! I felt that practitioners at SMZC were really living in harmony with all beings in this natural setting.

I was struck as I realized that the turkeys did not know that they were wild turkeys. A wild turkey is 100 percent wild turkey, but it doesn't know that, even in a dream. It is just being and doing a wild turkey with its whole being, without any thought. The wild turkey does not know how important it is in the human world, especially around the time of Thanksgiving.

The wild turkeys don't worry about being caught by human beings, cooked and eaten with joy and gratitude. They do not know the story about the early European settlers and wild turkeys. They are simply real wild turkeys. The name, the story, and evaluation are only within the world of the human thinking mind.

Just like the real turkeys, in zazen we go beyond the artificial world of definition, comparison, conceptualization, and evaluation.

In *Mind Sky*, each discourse is shining clearly, and all the discourses reflect each other, like the mani-jewels in Indra's Net. Shunryu Suzuki-roshi is still alive within this network of bright jewels; his legacy is carried on in Jakusho Kwong-roshi's teachings.

Shohaku Okumura

EDITOR'S PREFACE

Sonoma Mountain is an ancient mountain, known to be a place of great spiritual power. This feeling is palpable. The ground of Sonoma Mountain Zen Center speaks the Dharma directly—simply to enter the zendo is to breathe its essence intimately. But really, it is everywhere. Of the Zen Center itself, one can say that the whole place is the practice.

Sonoma Mountain Zen Center's true temple name is *Genjo-ji*. Kwong-roshi says that "*Genjo* can be translated as 'being here in the present moment,' or 'the actualization of this moment.' Zen asks you to be here *within* this moment, to recognize that you and this moment are not separate."

Long ago, when I first visited Sonoma Mountain Zen Center, it was just that: an overnight visit. When I finally found my way back, it was with firm intention. This time I stayed.

Early on, Roshi's greeting to me as I was filling out the membership form was "Watch out—don't get caught!" but it was already too late. I was hooked. In Jakusho Kwong I found my teacher, heir to Shunryu Suzuki and a true Soto Zen master. In his low-key, unassuming manner, Jakusho Kwong expresses not only deep wisdom, but also always a sense of wonder and childlike enthusiasm.

An artist rather than a scholar, he expresses himself most vividly in his unique calligraphy.

Kwong-roshi's memorable talks, or *teishos*, are often discursive, at times sounding like random free association. But underneath, these tangential threads are skillfully woven together, and their interconnectedness is clear.

Adapting them for the written page and editing them was challenging. In doing so, I nonetheless hoped to keep the original flavor, the essence of Jakusho Kwong-roshi.

It has been a rare privilege to work with Roshi on *Mind Sky*. The entire process has been a teaching.

Despite editorial nitpicking about syntax and word usage, our many meetings have been inspiring—and a great deal of fun! Roshi has a great sense of humor, so there have been many detours as he's shared stories and photographs—lots of recollections, anecdotes, and lots of laughter. I leave every meeting happy and with renewed energy.

He manifests *prajna* awareness in all his actions and in his sense of detail—his precise placement of objects, whether in *oryoki* setting or simply placing shoes together on the floor ("so they won't feel lonely")—showing his care and respect for all things: each thing is of equal value.

I remember once trying to straighten the framed picture of our Third Ancestor hanging behind our zendo altar. Walking by, Roshi laughed and said, "You'll never do it!"—as the vertical redwood wall boards of the original barn, over a hundred years old, are not always quite perpendicular.

A true bodhisattva, Kwong-roshi has shown me infinite compassion, loving-kindness, patience, and generosity. With infinite gratitude, I bow deeply to you, Roshi.

I also want to thank all the sangha members for their encouragement, and particularly those who have helped me on this project: thanks to Neil Meyer, for the work he did before me, and for his trenchant critiques. Thanks to readers Ed Cadman, Nancy Reder, and Peter Pocock, who copyedited much of the draft manuscript and made excellent suggestions along the way, and to Katsuzen King, editor of *Mountain Wind*, who also read and commented. I am grateful to you all for your efforts.

Thanks to Nyoze Kwong, for meticulously scanning all the calligraphy and photographs in this book, somehow finding time despite his many responsibilities.

Thanks to Tom Huffman for providing me with transportation as well as delivery service during the COVID-19 lockdown. This is *danaparamita*.

Thanks to Max, for bearing with me, and for helping with computer glitches.

And to my very dear old friend Ike Williams—thanks for coming out of retirement to give expert counsel, pro bono.

Much of this book was completed before the COVID-19 pandemic, which forced Sonoma Mountain Zen Center to close to the public. During this period, many ongoing programs and projects had to be postponed indefinitely as we were obliged to work remotely. Still, we continue, with residents as caretakers. Thanks to the tremendous efforts of Nyoze Kwong and the SMZC office, our programs have gone onto Zoom, with twice-daily zazen periods, *sesshins*, speakers, and participants from all over the world joining in. Despite the COVID-19 lockdown and financial hardship, the Zen Center is thriving.

Sally Scoville
Editor

AUTHOR'S PREFACE

FOLLOWING THE SUCCESS of *No Beginning, No End*, I was urged by many friends to do a second book. I first initiated this project almost ten years ago, but it was postponed because of other commitments.

Still, I returned to it, feeling the importance of transmitting the Dharma to a much wider audience—now possible, thanks to social media. In this way I carry on the directly transmitted teachings of my own teacher, Shunryu Suzuki-roshi.

Transmitting the Dharma is more urgent than ever now—with the climate crisis, the world in turmoil, and COVID-19 affecting us all. We should realize that we are not separate; we are interconnected with everyone, with all things. Right here, right now.

Mind Sky has come to fruition after many years of practice, study, and teaching—and thanks to the dedication of the students who worked on this project.

So many people have been instrumental in so many ways in the development of the book that it would be difficult to name them all.

First, I wish to acknowledge my teacher, Shunryu Suzuki-roshi, whose wisdom and compassion led me to Zen practice. Although I was with him for only eleven years before he died, his profound influence inspired me to build Sonoma Mountain Zen Center, Genjo-ji, in 1973 as a gesture of gratitude for his teaching. I feel his presence to this day, as we continue to practice here.

I acknowledge with deepest gratitude his influence and that of three other Zen teachers early on: Dainin Katagiri, Kobun Chino Otogawa, and Hoitsu Suzuki. I was blessed to have direct connections with many other teachers as well, including Taizan Maezumi, Kosho Uchiyama, Preah Maha Ghosananda, H. H. the Fourteenth Dalai Lama, Thich Nhat Hanh, Seung Sahn Sunim, Chögyam Trungpa, and Mitsu Suzuki, who all represent the spirit behind the words in this book.

I have great appreciation for the many Sonoma Mountain Zen Center sangha members who helped at different stages in the development of this project.

Thanks to all the students who transcribed these discourses, including Neil Meyers, Chuck Tensan Ramey, Tim Metzger, Ed Genzen Cadman, John Kaian Jennings, Kathy Dennison, Fern LaRocca, Sophia Close, and Sally Scoville. My thanks to Jundo Farrand, Choan Atwell, and others who recorded Dharma talks in the zendo, and to Dan Landault for converting earlier talks to digital format. I am grateful to Katsuzen King and Neil Meyers for careful verification of quotations, sources, and references.

I can never adequately acknowledge the contributions made by my wife, Shinko—as my lifelong partner, senior student, and cofounder of Sonoma Mountain Zen Center. She has been selflessly at my side, always.

Thanks to my son and co-abbot, Nyoze, and his wife, Kashin, who are beyond any dreams as they continue to maintain our Soto Zen heritage. They are exemplars of the true spirit of practice at Genjo-ji. And thanks to my other three sons: Ryokan and Cam Shunryu have helped greatly in redefining the Zen Center's operations during the COVID crisis and beyond, while Evri practices his art and teaches art as well. We all live near each other and are in close contact.

Last but not least, thanks to my editor, longtime student, and former SMZC resident Sally Myogetsu Scoville.

Though Neil Meyers had worked on editing transcripts in the early stages of this project, he had since retired. Some ten years later, it seemed as if no one in the sangha would be able to undertake the job of editing this book and seeing it through to completion. Finally, in January 2018, Sally stepped up to the plate and took on the challenge.

She worked wholeheartedly and tirelessly on this project for three years, first culling more than fifty transcripts—thousands of pages— and then selecting thirty to translate into the material that would become this book. She crafted and edited all the chapters, revising and fine-tuning each one with me. She was indefatigable, asking questions, verifying quotes and sources; and she persisted, patiently prodding me to continue, and urging me on to the end.

Sally was ably assisted by readers Ed Cadman, Peter Pocock, and Nancy Reder, who copyedited and offered valuable suggestions.

In addition, Sally was instrumental in finding the ideal publisher for *Mind Sky* in Wisdom Publications, and for coordinating communications with them to see this book come to fruition.

My deepest gratitude goes to Sally for her work on this project.

I have great appreciaton for Ben Gleason, my editor at Wisdom, who edited the manuscript with scrupulous attention to detail and shepherded production of the entire book. *Mind Sky* would not have been published without him. I also appreciate the work of Laura Cunningham, and proofreader Gretchen Gordon.

Many thanks to Gopa Campbell for book design, and to Kat Davis for coordinating the cover design of *Mind Sky*, which turned out beyond my expectations.

J.K.

EMPTYING
INTO SPACIOUSNESS

As we merge sound, breath, and air,
we're emptying into spaciousness.
—DOGEN

PEOPLE OFTEN ASK me about the distinction between Zen and mindfulness meditation. Zen practice— *zazen* meditation— may seem difficult and intimidating compared to mindfulness meditation. But put simply, it goes beyond the *samadhi* of mindfulness. In zazen, *samadhi* eventually leads to *shikantaza*—which means "just sitting."

Shikantaza is objectless meditation, in which we don't concentrate on any object or goal, or expect any gain. We let go of thoughts. We are just sitting.

Our great ancestor Dogen gave instructions in his essay "Fukanza-zengi" for what to do with the mind in zazen: "Think of not-thinking. How do you think of not-thinking? Nonthinking. This in itself is the essential art of zazen."

This quotation refers to a story about Yakusan Igen (Ch. Yaoshan Weiyan), who lived in eighth-century China. Yakusan was Sekito Kisen's disciple. One day after Yakusan had finished zazen, a monk asked him, "What are you thinking of in the immoveable, mountain-like state of zazen?" Yakusan replied, "I think of not-thinking." The monk asked, "How can one think of not-thinking?" Yakusan answered, "By nonthinking."

Living in this troubling and chaotic world profoundly affects everyone's well-being. Do you have to be continually stressed out and hurried? Is there a choice? An alternative?

Can you just sit down and give your mind a rest in meditation?

Mindfulness meditation has really helped a lot of people with stress reduction and pain management. But there can also be great misuse of mindfulness. In Buddhism, mindfulness or insight meditation—*vipassana*—is the Theravada tradition of calming the body and mind. The misuse of mindfulness is that, without a spiritual basis, people may hope to be acquiring something. In mindfulness, instead of giving something up, there can be a goal of gaining something, like relief from stress or chronic pain—or blissful happiness. I think we have to be careful about this.

People find that this form of meditation is a way to ease anxiety and stress, and it has become hugely popular and widespread. Ever since *Time* magazine devoted its cover and a full issue to the "Mindfulness Revolution" in 2014, there have been endless articles and bestselling books—even monthly magazines—devoted to the subject of mindfulness. But without some spiritual foundation, meditation practice doesn't go very far. Mindfulness programs are marketed commercially and are found in large corporations, public schools, and government agencies. Corporate mindfulness programs are intended, essentially, to increase workers' productivity through stress reduction. Mindfulness has become commodified to such an extent that I am reluctant now even to use the term.

The primary focus of Zen practice is on sitting meditation—zazen. The kanji for *zazen* (座禅) shows two people sitting together on the ground. *Za* means "to sit" and *zen* simply means "meditation." You can start sitting zazen at any age, but it is easier when you're young and your body is flexible enough to sit in the lotus posture or cross-legged. If you have physical difficulties, of course you can sit in a chair.

A while ago a new student here told me, "Coming here to practice didn't change my life. I just discovered what I already have." This is the essential point. Each one of you already has what's needed, but you do not realize it. I don't know how long it takes to feel confident about your fundamental buddha-nature, which is present right now. It's not something you learn in school. You were born with it, fully developed, waiting to be realized. It is with you perpetually. As Suzuki-roshi said, "Everywhere you go, it's always with you. It hasn't left you for one minute." But it seems that of all the species in the animal kingdom, only human beings fail to know this intuitively.

In meditation, it's common to try to stop the mind's activity entirely. That is actually the worst thing to do, because the result is invariably more activity. There's nothing wrong with coming to meditation in order to quiet the mind, but since trying to stop the mind during meditation is impossible, what you need to do is let it pervade your whole body. This is because any active mind, whether preoccupied or disturbed, keeps telling you that you should be *doing* something. As your mind becomes busier it seems to set off an alarm, insisting that you pay attention. What you can do is to focus not with the brain-mind but with the body-mind.

In zazen, this attention to body-mind eventually leads to an expanded awareness both of your own body and of the entire universe in which it exists. When mind truly permeates body, you are concentrating neither on inside nor outside, nor in between. Rather, your concentration permeates your whole body. This means that the mind itself is fundamentally uninterrupted and capable of reaching through the entire universe.

I think of zazen as slowly unwinding a ball of yarn with your full attention. If you do it impatiently, you'll leave plenty of knots, and you'll still have to untangle them carefully. In fact, you'll meet all kinds of delusions through the unwinding process of zazen. No other way is so direct. It's the most reliable method for confronting and working with what's in your mind—the chatter, the projections, the fears. Since your mind is with you wherever you go, you need to sit down and start unwinding your ball of yarn. It's your life. No one can do this for you. Your teacher can set you in a particular direction, but you have to go on the path alone.

If you decide to do zazen every day, then do it every day; if once a week, do it once a week! Try to sit at the same time every day, so that it forms a consistent rhythm in your life. Don't begin missing it. This discipline may be hard if you're alone; it helps to sit with others—in a community, a sangha.

The greatest challenge in zazen is your conceptualizing mind, which accelerates endlessly, from the moment you get up to when you go to sleep. Often there's hardly an instant in twenty-four hours when you're not furiously thinking. Unless you have a way to appease the incessant chatter, you can end up being completely driven to distraction by delusive thoughts.

You don't escape from your delusions in zazen. Instead, you look straight at them, since you have to work with them. This is the paradox. You never enter a promised paradise in which there will be no delusion. But all your delusions are workable. If they weren't, I think we'd all go mad. Still, you need to work with them in the right way. As Zen students, you should be totally committed to sitting—as Dogen put it, sitting wholeheartedly.

When you're wholeheartedly practicing zazen, you're not "doing" zazen. You're not doing anything, because the thinking mind has ceased. You're not "doing" at all anymore. That's what "wholehearted" means. There's a big difference right here. Even if your wholeheartedness lasts for a single second, this is the cessation of thought. *You're* not doing zazen; zazen is doing *you*. Zazen is doing zazen.

In Japan, after a fall planting of wheat, farmers used to go into the fields and trample down whole acres of the young green stalks to make the crop stronger. The growing stalks would come back up even sturdier, and thus result in an abundant harvest.

This is like what we do in practicing zazen. Trampling down the growing crop is really a metaphor for trampling down our egos. Like inattentive farmers whose crops fail, we will find that our spiritual selves won't ripen if we make no effort in our practice. We have to crush our egos, over and over again, until our delusions dissolve as they appear.

When we sit in zazen, our hands form what's known as the cosmic *mudra*—left hand over right, thumb tips touching—which rests not in the lap but against the belly, encircling and enshrining the *tanden* area— that is, the energy field right below the navel. By resting our thinking mind in the palm of our left hand, and forming this mudra with our whole mind, we can feel and enjoy the lengthening of our spine as we sit upright. Holding this mudra against the *tanden*, we are actually holding the universe. And as we hold this mudra it holds us too.

It requires effort, this mudra. You have to work on it. Usually when you work on something, you think you're working on *it*, but actually it is working on *you*. Have you ever thought of it this way? When you try to wrap your thinking mind around something, it's working on you. Just relax a bit, instead of anticipating what happens next.

There will be a love-hate relationship with this mudra. You'll love it when it feels good but you'll hate it when your shoulders are aching. And this may go on for some time until it finds its place. When you feel sleepy, keep your eyes open and push the mudra against your *tanden*. There's strength in this. Breathe from the *tanden* as well as through the nose. Breathing through the *tanden* connects you to the universe. Observe your breath: be aware of how you regulate it and how you use it, in everything you do. You'll find a big difference—like night and day. When you breathe this way, it cuts through your thinking. Then when you do think, your thinking will be focused, clear, and sharp. You'll enjoy it.

Breathing should sound like the wind. If we listen to our breath instead of our thinking mind, and hear our own breathing, then we have gone *behind* our thinking. Hearing our breath like the wind gives us a sense of wonder as we inhale and exhale thousands of times each day. And if we put the emphasis especially on the exhalation, then our breath, sounding like the wind, merges into sheer spaciousness. At the same time, we still hear external sounds—like birdsong outside—and our meditation practice can begin to feel as if it embraces everything.

In Zen meditation, we're not trying to exclude anything. We could say that as we merge breath, body, and mind we're emptying into spaciousness. We are focused no longer on our thinking mind, but on the natural sound of our breathing itself. In this way we can enjoy the stability of our body, its sensory capacities, its sheer presence. When our mind pervades our body, we instinctively follow the natural fluency of our breath.

In zazen, *samadhi* eventually leads to *shikantaza*—just sitting. It's actually becoming very still and doing nothing. Just sitting, that's all, remaining disinterested in the incessant chatter of the thinking mind, which seems to go on forever. At least once in a twenty-four-hour day, we can disengage from the usual interior dialogue that leads from one thought to another and another.

This disengagement is the purpose of *shikantaza*. In *shikantaza* we are just sitting quietly, aware of sounds, especially of the sound of the breath during exhalation. *Shikan* means "directly" or "just." *Ta* is "to strike or hit" and *za* is "to sit": literally, "hit-sit." "Hit-sit" suggests something viscerally, physically present. The instant you hit something you merge with it; in *shikantaza* you not only become one with sitting, you *are* the sitting. There's no dualism in "hit-sit," no gap between subject and object. This is *prajna*, or inherent wisdom. To experience this, even for just a moment, is to witness profound simplicity, utterly without embellishment. What could be simpler than just sitting down, not doing anything? You feel fluidity, warmth in your heart, body, and hands. To experience this isn't shattering or mind-blowing, but you are totally alive in the present moment. In *shikantaza* there's no past, no future—maybe not even a present. We just sit from moment to moment to moment. Simply breathing quietly—fully aware and alert, our energy surging within— we touch our true life force.

The twelfth-century Zen master Wanshi (Ch. Hongzhi Zhengjue) used the term *silent illumination* for what happens in "just sitting." Although it may sound inactive, silent illumination has great energy. You're not a lump of flesh. You're silently illuminating, emanating pure fiery energy, which consumes the deeply rooted greed, anger, and ignorance keeping you separated from reality. Once these delusions are extinguished there is no obstacle to seeing the basic goodness that is already there within you.

In his verse "The Acupuncture Needle of Zazen," Wanshi speaks of "illuminating without encountering objects." We may assume that every object we encounter is delusion, but Wanshi's phrase implies that there is no object. To understand this, we need to ask: What is the essence of this object? What is it that we see? *Who* is it that sees? We need to investigate what's behind the object, and behind that, and further behind, until there is no behind. Wanshi also says that we must do so without grasping, without reaching toward something outside ourselves. We don't need to touch what we already have. That effort would be extra. This dynamic awareness is present, in our knowing without touching, without engaging in discriminating thinking. Dualism is dissolved.

This, rather than any suppression of thought, is *prajna* awareness. Although it may be difficult to perceive, "illuminating without encountering objects" is exactly what occurs in true meditation practice. Illuminating without encountering objects: once you become thoroughly aware of this in zazen, there's no need to come to a Zen center. It's no longer a matter of seeking assurance, but of manifesting your own wisdom and transmitting it to others. I'm really just selling water by the river.

Wanshi comments: "If you think you have cut off the illusory mind or the deluded mind instead of *clarifying* how the delusion mind melts, delusion mind will come up again as though you had not cut the root of a blade of grass." Wanshi is saying that rather than trying to cut off delusory mind, you should come to see how delusions vanish in the light of *prajna* awareness. Otherwise your delusory mind will come up again and again, as though you'd cut the stem of a plant but let the root survive. Wanshi's objectless illumination doesn't deny the objective reality of your experiences, but allows them to merge naturally into unified awareness, into *prajna*.

This cutting of the root reminds me of a story of three monks of the three main Buddhadharma schools—Theravada, Mahayana, and Vajrayana.

There is a poisonous plant growing by the side of the road where the three monks are traveling. The Theravadan monk notices it and places a stone on it, hoping that it will die before anyone touches it. This is an implicit comment on the Theravadan method of meditation: here, if one has strong corporeal desire, one contemplates decay, death, and extinction to kill the desire, rather than trying to get at the cause of the desire. The Mahayana monk cuts the plant off at the ground, thus removing the immediate danger. However, the roots are still there: the poisonous plant will grow back and have to be cut again. From a Zen standpoint, this means that even after enlightenment delusions will continue to arise. The Vajrayana monk pulls up the whole plant, knowing that if he cooks it its properties will be transformed and it will turn into beneficial medicine. The dilemma here is how to do away with delusion—with the stone, at the root, or with medicine?

In his "Song of the Grass-Roof Hermitage," Sekito Kisen tells us to turn around the light—to turn awareness around to shine within, and then just return. In the same way, Wanshi urges practitioners to take the backward step, and stand directly in the middle of the circle where light issues forth. Wanshi and Sekito Kisen are both predecessors of Dogen. For them, it's not an assumption but reality that we are each in the circle, in the presence of light, whether we see it or not.

If you allow everything to drop away, realization may occur. It is usually not earth-shattering at all, however, just great simplicity in turning your light to shine within. You take your mind just as it is, in whatever state it's in, and focus on it—shine your awareness on it. It's mind on mind. That's the backward step. This practice takes time, so you shouldn't get discouraged if you do not get it right away. It requires discipline and training to turn your light to shine within. Direct your attention and closely observe your own awareness.

Ask yourself, where is my awareness, right now?

You can't study Zen just by reading and thinking about it; intellectual understanding is not Zen. So many books have been written on Zen Buddhism—such a prolific body of literature about something you can't even talk about! If you read them all, it would consume your whole life, and you'd still miss the point.

So stop your practice based on "pursuing words and following after speech," as Dogen puts it. Don't let yourself become attached to words. Words just point the way. Learn to take the backward step that turns your light inward, illuminating your true self. Then, without a doubt, your original face, your original mind, will appear.

WAY-SEEKING MIND

*A comparison between awakening the way-seeking mind
and enlightenment is like that between the light generated
by a firefly and that of a vast raging fire.*
—DOGEN

ZEN CONSTANTLY APPEARS and reappears. While we study
it, it can seem distant from the deepest feelings that originally
aroused our commitment. My teacher, Shunryu Suzuki-roshi,
would refer to this fluctuation as an occurrence of the "way-seeking
mind." This was a phrase I hadn't heard before. Normally awakening
and enlightenment are associated with "bodhi-mind," but Suzuki-roshi
talked more often about "way-seeking mind."

Whenever I heard Suzuki-roshi use this phrase, it made me trem-
ble inside. I don't know what it was, but the phrase aroused something
primordial in me, beyond any thought of religion or philosophy. I now
realize that he was speaking not only of a Mahayana principle, but also
of an actual human feeling of profound intimacy.

In one of the early Buddhist sutras there's a fable about four kinds of
horses. First there's the finest, the champion horse. Then there's the second best, a good one; then the third, a poor one; and finally the last, the

worst. The best, the keenest horse will run slow or fast, to the right or left, at the rider's will, before it sees the shadow of the whip; the second best will run as well as the first one does, just before the whip touches its skin; the third one will run when feeling pain on its body; but the fourth horse must be struck again and again until the pain penetrates to the marrow of its bones before it moves.

Naturally, when I heard Suzuki-roshi tell this story, I wanted to be the first horse! I think this is common; we all want to be the best, and if we can't be, sometimes only the next best will do.

This illustrates clearly the difficulty of Zen practice. Nobody has an easy time with zazen practice at the outset; those who say they do are probably deceiving themselves. Suzuki-roshi comments, "You may think that when you sit in zazen, you will find out whether you are one of the best horses or one of the worst. This, however, is a misunderstanding of Zen."

I certainly had this misunderstanding, and you may too. But if you think about it, Suzuki-roshi's point is clear. As he explains, "If you think the purpose of Zen practice is to train you to become one of the best horses, you will have a big problem. This is not the right understanding. If you practice Zen correctly, it doesn't matter if you are the best horse or the worst one. When you consider the mercy of Buddha, how do you think Buddha will feel about the four kinds of horses? He will have more sympathy for the worst one than for the best one."

When you're determined to sit with the great mind of Buddha, you'll realize that being the worst is the most useful. The struggle itself is inherently relentless, but it means you are actively participating in loss. Your legs may hurt, and you may be exhausted, but what matters is your active participation in loss.

The term *way-seeking mind* is at the heart of the Mahayana tradition. It includes our willingness to sacrifice, to forsake perfect enlightenment for the sake of others. And, through the struggle that this involves, we

Young Jakusho Kwong with Shunryu Suzuki-roshi

identify with all who experience similar difficulties—in fact, ours may often be far smaller in comparison.

Eihei Dogen, the thirteenth-century founder of Soto Zen and author of the great *Shobogenzo*, describes three kinds of mind. The first, *citta*, is thinking mind, discriminating mind. The next is *hridaya*, or heart—the mind of grass and trees—meaning the instinctive mind, the pre-conscious life force. Third is *vriddha*, the matured, concentrated mind—that is, *prajna*, the mind of real wisdom, awareness of reality itself.

Paradoxically, it's discriminating mind that causes one to awaken to the way-seeking mind. Just as the lotus grows from mud, the way-seeking mind, aroused by *citta*, is able to rise from a state of delusion toward enlightened realization. This is the beauty of our practice. We don't dwell in the discriminating mind, but instead we utilize it for enlightenment. At the same time, although we can't awaken way-seeking mind without discriminating mind, these are not the same and should not be confused.

Dogen says that putting another person's enlightenment before one's own is the way of those who have awakened to the way-seeking mind. But note that the way-seeking mind is not innate, nor does it suddenly appear out of the blue. It arises as the gradual result of a spiritual link between ourselves and the Buddha.

This spiritual link depends on what's called *sati*, the Pali word for mindfulness, which is the strong foundation developed in zazen. You can sense it when you're sitting quietly enough to recall the original "knower" within yourself. Then comes the unwavering attention, the *samadhi* that joins with *prajna*, wisdom. However, it takes disciplined practice for this spiritual linking to occur. Dogen points out that the way-seeking mind cannot be transmitted, even by bodhisattvas. Nor can it be induced by deliberate effort in sitting zazen. What is essential is great faith. In sailing, you'll aim your boat in the right direction; at some point, you may have to let go of the tiller and oars. It all comes down to this: letting go. There may be no wind, you may have no oars—but at some point you'll just have to trust a greater power beyond your own effort. You need to have abiding faith in something greater than your ordinary self. Something universal.

Dogen points out that people who have awakened to the way-seeking mind may practice for innumerable eons before they either become buddhas or remain to help others find the way. Using right speech, action, and thought as the means of arousing the way-seeking mind in others is the way of all who have themselves awakened to bodhi-mind. He says that a comparison between first awakening the way-seeking mind and enlightenment is like that between the light generated by a firefly and that of a vast raging fire, but this immense difference immediately disappears once those who have awakened to the way-seeking mind also vow to promote the enlightenment of others before their own. Dogen is emphatic about the importance of this pivotal Mahayana principle.

The moment we undertake to help others before we consider our own salvation, the discriminating mind becomes transformed into the way-seeking mind. When we awaken the way-seeking mind, even if only for an instant, all things become conducive to its growth. We choose to give up the usual inclination to consider ourselves first. We act spontaneously, with genuine altruism, to benefit others. This selfless compassion marks the true way-seeking mind.

Once the way-seeking mind is awakened, our life is wholly transformed. We are no longer living in opposition to the objective world. Further, we see that the way-seeking mind is inextricably involved with the impermanence of all things.

Awakening the way-seeking mind and experiencing enlightenment may occur and vanish in an instant. If this were not so, past wrongs could not disappear and subsequent good actions could not appear as they do, moment by moment. Only the Buddha Tathagata understands this fully, for it is only he who can utter an entire sutra in an instant.

With the passing of each instant, we undergo incessant existing and nonexisting. In the time it takes an average person to snap their fingers, sixty-five such instants pass.

We're like strobe lights flashing on and off. So is the whole universe! According to Dogen, one "instant" of time equals 0.075 of a second. That means quite a bit of activity in twenty-four hours! Existing, nonexisting, existing, nonexisting, and existing. This is the fundamental, impermanent nature of our minds and our lives.

JUST SITTING

WHY IS IT so difficult to realize your true nature? It's because your mind is distracted by incessant thoughts, delusive thinking. You should let go of your assumption of self—let go of these thoughts. This letting-go is a result of intense, continuous zazen practice. The longer you practice and study Zen, the deeper your understanding becomes.

This resembles what happens in meditation: when self vanishes it is in a state of nondoing. This is what develops with Zen training. Whatever thinking you *think* you need to do can be postponed until the meditation period has ended. The reality is that you are only facing the wall in front of you. That's the wonder of of zazen practice—you are awake and alert, and you are just sitting.

Skeptics ask, is there really any point in sitting zazen? What's the use? So here's a famous story about the eighth-century Chinese Chan master Baso (Ch. Mazu Daoyi).

> When Baso was a young student, his teacher, Nangaku (Ch. Nanyue Huairang), happened to pass the hut where he was sitting zazen.
>
> Nangaku poked his head through the door and asked, "What have you been doing recently?"

Baso replied, "Recently I have been practicing seated meditation exclusively." Nangaku asked him, "And what is the aim of your seated meditation?"

Baso answered, "The aim of my seated meditation is to achieve Buddhahood."

Nangaku picked up a roof tile from the ground and began rubbing it vigorously.

On seeing this, Baso asked him, "Reverend monk, what are you doing?"

Nangaku replied, "I am polishing a tile."

Baso then asked, "What are you going to make by polishing a tile?"

Nangaku replied, "I am polishing it to make a mirror."

Baso said, "How can you possibly make a mirror by rubbing a tile?"

Nangaku replied, "How can you become a Buddha by practicing seated meditation?"

In the West, meditation is often thought of as simply quieting the mind. For instance, it's common to meditate before performing martial arts. But Zen meditation is much more profound. It entails realizing the true self, revealing the universe within. You must be careful to avoid practicing meditation with any goal of becoming a buddha. Whenever you sit in meditation you are already a buddha! There's a big difference between meditating to become a buddha and recognizing that you already are. The most important thing you can do is to awaken to your true nature, and then to continue practicing, compassionately and selflessly.

LEVELS OF AWARENESS

TRUE PEACE is beyond happiness or sadness. It's as vast and still as a calm sea. Such peace is expressed in the term *sati*, which haunted me when I first heard Suzuki-roshi describe it. *Sati* is not enlightenment, any more than *samadhi* or *prajna* are necessarily enlightenment. It's something that happens on the way. Actually, *sati* is the Pali word for mindfulness. But it is not simply about being mindful, or having a good memory.

Sati works on another level, in a different dimension for each of us. *Sati* is the deep composure prior to taking an action. Before the action is completed, 80 percent of it has been accomplished. It is the composure of a dancer before she performs on stage, or of a swimmer on the edge of the high-diving board—or even of a person at the point of death. There's a knower here. What they know is the deep peace found through zazen practice—a state of profound awareness, a spaciousness that includes everything.

This quality of awareness underlies basic Zen meditation. From Zen practice comes the realization of what we're doing, of how we treat others, and of how we treat ourselves. Reflective awareness is demanding. It reminds me of when I first heard someone talk enthusiastically about digital cameras, back in the early 1990s. When I saw the results, I was struck by how clear the photographs were—it was just like being right there! At the same time, I wondered whether such technology would take something away from the process involved with manual film cameras—loading the film, focusing, adjusting distance and aperture—all of which require focused attention and practice and patience. This process is so much like the practice of *sati* leading to *samadhi*, which leads to the inner world. That world may never be fully realized, but the process of reaching for it is important. So I thought I'd probably stick to the manual film camera, though it might be nice to have a digital camera and a smartphone too. The point is to use new technology rather than be used *by* it. We don't want to diminish the process that ignites our inner world and that protects the rich life force within us.

Sati appears as you invoke composure within yourself in zazen. It precedes *samadhi*, which is unwavering attention and concentration. *Sati* can take place anywhere. Someone recently told me about entering *sati* while working out on a treadmill! You need to be conscious of what you're doing, however, because the power of repetition entirely involves you, your body, and your breath. The characteristics of *sati* are steadiness and calm. In *sati* your presence is like a mountain. You don't fall down because you can't. You sit as still as a mountain, and in this stillness your mind develops unwavering attention. This can continue for a long time, until your deep reflective awareness emerges. At this point, there is not much to think about. This is *samadhi*.

I've met people so calm in their *samadhi* that they don't care to associate with anybody. They're so deeply attached to their tranquility that they prefer to be isolated from the external world. But we mustn't be so attached to that kind of *samadhi* where calmness is merely a matter of avoiding whatever makes us feel uneasy. In reality, actually dealing with the objective world is often frightening. In true *samadhi*, there's plenty of space to face such fear, especially when it's activated by questions like What is this? What's that noise? Who am I?

Once *samadhi* is enlarged this way, then our reflective awareness makes *prajna* possible, and there's no longer any need to think at all. At that point, we can be confident that our memory, our sense of self, won't turn to stone. Our *prajna* wisdom will blossom beyond the dualities and polarities that imprison us in our ordinary life. As *prajna* deepens further, we grow closer to what may be called enlightenment itself.

YOUNG DOGEN'S RESOLVE

If all human beings are born with buddha-nature,
why do we need to practice?

ORN IN 1200 CE, Eihei Dogen came from an aristocratic family; his father was a prominent figure in the imperial court. Dogen was two years old when his father died. His mother died a few years later, when the boy was only eight. Just before she left the physical world, she urged Dogen to become a monk. That was her last wish, and it deeply affected the young boy. It was said that during her funeral service, as he stood watching the incense smoke swirl up, he felt a profound sense of impermanence. Thus the young Dogen experienced firsthand the truth of impermanence and suffering.

If we don't truly understand impermanence, then we suffer. That glimpse of impermanence moved Dogen to enter the priesthood to study, taking the path that would lead him to become a great Zen master. Dogen lived during a time of upheaval in Japan, with constant political conflict between the emperor's government in Kyoto and the shogunate government in Kamakura, as well as widespread deadly epidemics and other natural disasters. But during this time a great cultural renaissance was beginning to emerge, and many Buddhist sects developed in this era.

In traditional mainstream Buddhism, it was believed that everyone has buddha-nature: you are born with it, and you will awaken to it. But Dogen called this doctrine into question. He first began practicing in the Tendai tradition in Kyoto, and was constantly questioning the other monks and teachers: "If we have the buddha-nature, why should we practice?" This question haunted him, but no one could give him a satisfactory answer. Consequently he left the Tendai monastery.

Dogen was eventually initiated and began studying with Myozen, a disciple of the Rinzai Zen master Eisai. At one point Dogen asked Myozen, "If we have the buddha-nature, then why do we have to practice?" And Myozen exclaimed, "Nobody knows!" He was repeating what the Chinese Zen master Nansen (Ch. Nanquan Puyuan) had once said to him: "Nobody knows. Only cats and white oxen."

This was Dogen's experience as he transmitted it to us. For him, "practice-realization" was not merely an abstract idea; it was his direct experience of reality.

Returning to Japan, Dogen announced, "I have come back empty-handed. I have realized only that my eyes are horizontal and my nose is vertical."

He soon founded the Japanese Soto school of Zen, introducing to Japan the *shikantaza* practice he had learned from Tendo Nyojo, who coined the term to refer to the Chan practice of silent illumination.

Eihei Dogen began writing the *Shobogenzo* (Treasury of the True Dharma Eye) soon after he returned from China to Japan. In fact, another Zen master, Daie (Ch. Dahui Zonggao), had already written a major work called *Shobogenzo*, but his teaching was the Rinzai view of Zen. Dogen, on purpose, took the title for his own magnum opus as a challenge to Daie. Dogen's teaching was *pure* Zen: *shikantaza*, or just sitting—silent illumination.

Daie was an outspoken critic of silent illumination; nonetheless, he was a close friend of Wanshi, who originated the practice of *shikantaza*.

Actually, before the *Shobogenzo*, Dogen had written the essay "Fukan-zazenji" (Universal Recommendation for Zazen), in which he gave his instructions for zazen, or upright sitting. These works are the heart and mind, the blood and guts, of Dogen's thinking. They are rooted in his personal experience, and express his own realization.

Rather than trying to convince us, in the *Shobogenzo* Dogen lays out the Dharma so that we can receive it in our own way, regardless of culture and tradition. Although it was written in the thirteenth century, it is still relevant to us now in the twenty-first century.

SHO · RIGHT
BO · DHARMA
GEN · REALIZE
ZO · TREASURE

PRESENTNESS

YOU MIGHT EXPECT zazen practice to be effective enough to end the pain in your knees if you were to sit zazen for two years. If this were your motivation, and I told you to practice for just two years, then you'd probably embrace zazen enthusiastically. But true practice is not just for two years, and it's not only for overcoming physical pain.

If I say that you need to practice for your whole life, you may be dismayed. But the Dharma is infinite. Just as there is no beginning and no end to the Dharma, so Zen practice is endless. Zen is with you wherever you go. Zen is life and life is Zen. It is the entire universe.

We're easily caught in the perpetual whirl of samsara. The purpose of zazen practice is to step away from this merry-go-round, and at the same time to recognize that the truth of the Dharma is to be revealed right in everyday living. It's not in your imagination. Where can you have a realization but exactly here, where you are right now? It is in the most inconspicuous occurrences in everyday life.

Zen Buddhism isn't perfect. If it were perfect, then in two years you would be assured of a great realization experience. That would be too easy! Many more people would be interested in it, and there would really be no need for me to teach. But because so many people get easily discouraged with Zen practice, and with their lives, I feel that I must keep on teaching Zen. That's why I continue, even as I grow old.

In fact, I became interested in Zen Buddhism precisely because there is no end to it. Even if all human beings were to vanish from this earth, the Dharma would still exist. There is no end to the Dharma—it is unborn, eternal, and infinite.

"Genjo Koan," one of the opening chapters of Dogen's great *Shobogenzo*, was first written in 1233 as a letter to a lay disciple, and it is pure poetry. If we look at the original Japanese manuscript, each sentence runs vertically, and they go from right to left. The second sentence is a mirror of the first, and the third and fourth sentences mirror each other. It's written in such a way that the phrase "When the use is large it is used largely" is one column, and "when the use is small it is used in a small way" is another, so that the two columns—that is, the two phrases—reflect each other.

While our eyes naturally take in the visual structure first, we see that the two columns look the same—the unconditioned mind does not discriminate between long and short words, between large and small. In our ordinary conditioned life, we tend to talk about good and bad, tall and short, major and minor—but actually, even the act of picking up a speck of dust can involve the same spirit as picking up a large stone. When we see things in the way Dogen urges us to, we needn't discriminate in our usual sense, because no comparison is possible.

How can we really judge something trivial against something important? As the "Sandokai" says, each thing has its own intrinsic virtue and nature.

The words *genjo koan* can be taken to mean variously "here and now," or "immediate presence," or even "presentness." At the same time, there's no end to our practice. In fact, one could say there's no end to our lives because there's no end to presentness itself.

Taizan Maezumi-roshi translated "Genjo Koan" as "The Way of

Everyday Life." This phrase reminds me of the terms *ji* and *ri*, often used in Zen to refer to the reality behind everything we see, hear, and think. *Ji* refers to the everyday world we generally see. *Ri*, denoting the unseen, gives us an important perspective we need to keep, since we usually interpret things only as *ji*. An odd Zen phrase, "breaking the skin born of your mother," suggests that we can realize our unborn nature through the dissolution of *ji* and *ri*.

"Genjo Koan" also reminds me of the saying "be here now," which became a catch phrase in the counterculture of the 1970s, when the late Ram Dass published his inspiring and seminal book, *Be Here Now*. His book has remained in print since its initial publication in 1971.

"Here and now" sounds good, but the reality is much more profound. In the foreground of our everyday life is the world of *ji*—"here." But *ri*, the unseen, exists behind it. *Ri* is the absolute of "now."

In a beautiful passage in "Genjo Koan" that uses the metaphors of a fish swimming in the ocean and a bird flying in the sky, Dogen illuminates the concepts of immediacy and endlessness:

> When a fish swims in the ocean, there is no end to the water, no matter how far it swims. When a bird flies in the sky, there is no end to the air, no matter how far it flies. However, the fish and the bird never leave their elements. When the use is large, it is used largely. When the use is small, it is used in a small way. Thus, no creature ever comes short of its own completeness. Wherever it stands, it does not fail to cover the ground. Though it flies everywhere, if the bird leaves the air, it will die at once. Water makes life and air makes life. The bird makes life and the fish makes life. Life makes the bird and life makes the fish. . . . If a bird or a fish tries to reach the end of its element before moving in it, this bird or this fish will not find

its way or its place. When we find our place at this moment, then practice follows and this is the realization of truth. For the place and the way are neither large nor small, neither subject nor object. They have not existed from the beginning, and they are not in the process of realization.

Dogen's point is that the fish and the bird never leave their elements. The fish swims in the ocean and the bird flies in the sky. What do human beings do? We don't leave our element either. Just as there's no end to the water as long as a fish swims in the ocean, there's no end to practice. Even if we once realize the truth, it's realization after realization; there's no end to it as long as we are still alive.

The term *endlessness* can be hard to relate to. When we find that in reality there is no beginning or end, it may cause anxiety and suffering, but in the context of Zen it means endless liberation, freedom—the freedom of a bird in soaring flight.

"Though the bird flies everywhere, if the bird leaves the air it will die at once."

We human beings may be able to go anywhere, thanks to technology, but we need to know how to go with our inherent *prajna* awareness— the mind that sees reality as it is—just as the bird knows instinctively where to fly. We must know what makes us truly alive; otherwise we will just die spiritually. Thousands, millions of people die every day, having lived lives of delusion, without ever realizing their original nature.

When we work at our ordinary jobs, we're generally aware of the passage of time, and when the day is over we just want to kick back and relax, but time keeps slipping away. However, the kind of time that brings true freedom has no goal, no end, just as there's no end to the Dharma or the truth. Zazen is not a means to an end.

The open space of zazen is a continuum. We normally divide space or time up—by calculating time, for example, in increments of hours, night and day, and past-present-future; or by measuring space as the distance between two points.

We are confined this way. But, after all, as Dogen said, "How far is the sky from the ground?" In the spaciousness of *samadhi*, there is no this and that, or here and there.

This open space remains continuous, even when we don't always feel it; it's all one space, one present time.

If there were a goal, then if you sat for two or three or four years you would be practically assured of becoming realized. But you first must abandon the conditioned idea that if you always do this then that will automatically happen, and within a certain time. The Dharma teaches that you have to give up such assumptions because they're obstructions to your seeing your inherent nature. They are in fact the conditions of your suffering.

Since all things have the same fundamental nature, when Dogen talks about a fish and a bird, he is speaking of us as well. In his sentence "when a fish swims in the ocean, there is no end to the water, no matter how far it swims," the "no end" applies to us, because when we're born into this world from mother and father, there is also something in us that is unborn. It's said that we actually die and are reborn 698,449,000 times while we are alive! This means that freedom is always possible, with every rebirth. There's no limit to the truth, which is as vast as the sky; there is no beginning or end to the Dharma.

This freedom from time and space can astonish us at times in our practice, when our sitting seems to go by in a second. Saying that "when a bird flies in the sky there's no end to the air, no matter how far it flies" also means that there's no limit to the truth. If "the fish and bird do not leave their elements," then a fish can never really be separated from the water, nor a bird from the air, without destroying themselves.

When Dogen adds, "no creature ever comes short of its own completeness," he is saying that we were all born with buddha-nature, and it has never left us for an instant. But although we are born already "complete," we need to discover this, to recognize it. We can do this only when we liberate ourselves from samsara.

From the perspective of Dharma activity, even seeming opposites are inseparable from each other. This is why, wherever we stand, we do not fail to cover the ground.

THE TEXTURE OF EMPTINESS

SUZUKI-ROSHI ONCE gave a particularly beautiful talk on Dogen's "Genjo Koan."

Genjo, like our temple name, means "everything" or "our everyday life." One meaning of *koan* is "first principle." *Genjo koan* means all the various activities by which our practice is extended from here to there—from first principles to everyday life, bridging our practice from inside the zendo to the world outside, so that the two are a single, continuous activity.

Suzuki-roshi's talk involved Ummon's (Ch. Yunmen Wenyan) question and the matter of the first principle. Ummon was a Chan master living in southern China in the tenth century, during a period of constant war and strife. Once Ummon questioned his assembly, "I don't ask you about fifteen days ago. But what about fifteen days hence?" He waited for a response, but since no one answered, he simply said, "Every day is a good day." This was his method and his first principle. Despite the immense physical and mental hardships of his time, his first principle was to notice that every day was a good day.

Suzuki-roshi remarked about this teaching, "Today does not become yesterday."

Or, as Dogen put it, "Today does not become tomorrow. Each day is its own past and future, and has its own absolute value."

Here is a passage from Suzuki-roshi's talk from the archives of San Francisco Zen Center:

Each existence, animate or inanimate, is changing every moment, night and day. The change is like flowing water, which never flows back, which reveals its true nature in its eternal travel. Water flowing and clouds drifting are similar to a well-trained old Zen monk. The true nature of water and clouds is like the determined, single-minded traveling monks, who do not even take off their traveling sandals while under the roofs of sages. Worldly pleasure, philosophical pursuit, or whimsical ideas do not interest the traveling monk. Sincere to his true nature, he does not want to be fat and idle. Such a monk does not care for hospitality, which would stop his travels. He recognizes as true friends only those who travel with him on the way. The idea of this kind of travel may make you feel lonely, sad, and even sometimes helpless.*

Rather than promising nirvana, Suzuki-roshi describes something that leaves you feeling lonely, sad, and even helpless. In Zen this is "seeing things *as they are*." "Seeing things as they are" is a Zen expression of seeing the ordinary—and at the same time, the ultimate reality. Long periods of zazen—in which nothing happens—may lead to boredom or anger, or just an urge to avoid whatever brings on that sadness and loneliness. However, in Zen, when you sit down to meditate, such sensations naturally come up. Zazen is truthful and direct, and you learn to accept these feelings as bumps in the road.

Just what is it to taste being lonely? Is it a thing? Are you afraid of it? Can you touch it? What is it like to let yourself just be with it?

*From a talk by Suzuki-roshi, from the San Francisco Zen Center archives, date unknown.

What about boredom? Is that also something you want to avoid? You know, when you were a child, how you must have felt bored at times. Remember complaining, "There's nothing to do! When are we going to get there?" No entertainment! Now kids don't complain so much. That's because everyone—kids and adults alike—has smartphones, video games, Facebook, and so on. Constant entertainment, no problem! Constant distraction, certainly. These devices take you away from contact with your real self. It's OK to enjoy them, but you shouldn't become addicted to them so that they rule your life. Take a break!

In a seven-day silent *sesshin* retreat, boredom and fatigue may arise, but in the end, the realization of endlessness can touch the heart. In fact, if one doesn't practice wholeheartedly, the *sesshin* may seem pointless. What is it for?

It is in this endless practice that we can manifest the original purity that's always within us. Sitting in zazen hour after hour, when nothing seems to happen, may seem monotonous and boring, or one may feel sadness or loneliness, even anger, but stay with it. Boredom, sadness, loneliness, anger—these are all just words that express our underlying emotions. There's something wondrous behind these feelings.

Dogen suggests that we are endowed with bodhi-mind, but simply aren't yet aware of it. Dogen often talks about the evanescence of life, saying that life is "fading quickly." Awareness of this should make us realize how precious our lives are. To see that we're constantly fading, fading, fading away should make us feel enormous gratitude for life. This is so important. We need to fully understand our evanescence, this perpetual flashing on and off of light.

Interestingly, Suzuki-roshi pointed out that when Dogen talks about evanescence, he also mentions exhaling. I don't know how many times you exhale and inhale in one day, but breathing is of primary importance in zazen practice. If you truly notice yourself exhaling and inhaling, you'll realize there is no self. Interior and exterior aren't separate. Suzuki-roshi said that your throat is like a swinging door. There's no inside and no outside. It's all space. You're inside this room here, but outside there's the same space. It's all space. Space pervades everywhere.

So, it's most important to be aware of your breathing—especially to hear the sound of your breath rather than the noise of your thinking. When you breathe in zazen, you should draw your breath from the *tanden*—the energy point of your body, three finger-widths beneath the navel, which demands that your whole body breathe. Breathe this way in zazen; the sound of your breath will determine the strength of your sitting.

When you breathe like this, your breathing begins breathing you. With training, your breath will sound just like the wind—which means the self is dissolving. Then the mind is empty of thought. Breath controls mind; mind controls body.

What is this breathing? It's not you and it's not air. In Suzuki-roshi's words, "What is it that is not self at all? When you are completely involved in breathing there is no self."

In a Zen context, the stark word *emptiness* may sound alarming, but it simply means there's no gain in zazen. There is nothing *to* gain. Just with this natural rhythm of breathing, exhaling and inhaling, you will slowly enter a wonderful, wondrous place, where there's no thinking—which means no self. There's no self. That may sound frightening, but another Zen term for it is "no mind" or "empty mind."

If you think of an empty bottle, it doesn't mean that the bottle is gone; it's just empty. The mind, your mind, is still there, but it's absolutely free from the thought of self.

Most practices and beliefs have a beginning, a middle, and at the end a goal. But in Zen, since there's no end, there is no goal, no promise. To the question "If I do this, will that happen?" there is no sure answer. Endlessness means that the Dharma never began. It was not created. The Dharma is infinitely spacious.

MOMENT TO MOMENT

IT'S WINTER NOW here in northern California. As I was walking home a few nights ago, I was struck by how lucky we are to breathe pure air here, to see this whole great canopy of stars flashing, thousands of millions of miles away. It's Indra's net! A sense of wonder and gratitude touched my heart. When the heart is touched it's a moment of purity. Even at my age, that purity is still there.

Suzuki-roshi once said that if it's dark and you want to find your keys, you have to see with your fingertips, with your whole attention, with a purity that is clear and bright. Looking for something in the dark is no different from seeing life as it is, if you're entirely present. You need to stay completely open as you search for your keys. If you aren't in a hurry, your fingers will "see" different things—feeling the wood of the table, the smoothness of a stone. If you aren't impatient, and your mind is fully functioning, it will be the *prajna* awareness—what Suzuki-roshi called Big Mind—that sees reality as it is. This is a forgotten function that everyone has. To realize this is no more than looking for something in the dark.

You should remember that your *prajna* awareness has always existed fully developed. It will not expand or dwindle. It was here when you were born and will be here after you die. What is important is to recognize what you have inherently; it is with you wherever you go. You may become distracted and discouraged, but wholehearted Zen practice reminds you that you already have this profound inner purity.

When you take a long hike in the forest and happen to pick up a leaf to look at it closely, you're not judging; you're just examining it, exploring the veins in the leaf and its shape. At such a moment, the discriminating mind isn't there. You're not thinking that you dislike this particular kind of leaf, or wish it could be greener. You've picked it up without thought, and you're seeing it *as it is*. This is the *prajna* awareness—your Zen mind—that is behind your conceptual mind.

There is a Zen phrase, "Only don't know." *Prajna* awareness is the don't-know mind. Only at the end of conceptual thought does one cross a threshold of wonder, beyond the thinking mind. It's like seeing into the vastness of the night sky.

During my training, Suzuki-roshi often reminded me that it was more important to practice the Buddhadharma from moment to moment than to think about becoming enlightened. The problem was my gaining mind, as I would discover. I was not aware then that practice itself is realization.

Once in the early 1960s I heard that the Soto Zen archbishop of North America, Yamada Sokan, was coming to visit us at Soko-ji Zen Center in San Francisco. Being young and impressionable, I was excited, since this was our first visit from such a venerable Zen master. In preparing for the visit, Suzuki-roshi decided that to honor the bishop he would practice traditional *takahatsu*—alms begging—in San Francisco's busy Fillmore District. He would put on the straw begging hat that almost completely concealed his face. Wearing his robe, with white cotton gloves covering his hands, he would be totally anonymous. He would carry a begging bowl and a tall staff I had carved for him with rings that jingled as he walked. Imagine this, right in the middle of San Francisco!

We were eager to accompany Suzuki-roshi, but he told us he had to go alone. He returned with his begging bowl containing just three silver quarters and a grapefruit. In this way he demonstrated that instead of trying to become enlightened, the important thing is to practice just as we are, from moment to moment, because everything that happens is moment to moment.

So where are you, moment to moment?

Right now ... BAM!* ... right here ... BAM!

*Strikes the floor with his stick.—Ed.

ONE UNBROKEN MOMENT

The ultimate nature of physical reality is not a collection
of separate objects, but an undivided whole that is
in a constant state of flow and change.

I ONCE FOUND AN odd definition of *one* as "the lesser cardinal number," but to me it is not comparative—it's not lesser or greater than something else. *One* suggests what is incomparable. When we say we are all one, we may mean that we're all one world. From a Buddhist standpoint, we are all sentient beings, ignorant and deluded. But that we're *one* also means that every sentient being is originally a buddha, and we can be enlightened by the very delusion that defines us. That delusion itself can be the source of our enlightenment, our liberation. Once realized, these two are known to come from the same sourcelessness.

If we recognize that the ultimate nature of all dharmas isn't a collection of separate objects as they appear to us, but actually an undivided whole, can we then truly divide up anything we experience—the sky, or night and day? In a sense this is exactly what we are conditioned to do without realizing it, and that's why we suffer and cause suffering.

We may shrink back if we see a person on the street acting strangely, just because they don't look OK—but they may be a buddha. Our habits of discrimination, of avoiding situations we think unpleasant or challenging, are mostly attempts to alleviate our own suffering. In fact, just as we are faced with unpleasant problems, we'll meet that peculiar-looking person again and again until we finally begin to understand how to respond—with compassion and insight. This is *upaya*—skillful means.

The renowned theoretical physicist David Bohm once engaged in dialogues with noted spiritual teachers about questions he couldn't answer through science. He suggested that the ultimate nature of physical reality is not a collection of separate objects as they appear to us, but an undivided whole that is in perpetual and dynamic flux. He posited that quantum physics and relativity theory point to a universe in which all parts merge into one totality, which is in a constant state of flow and change.

This is precisely the Dharma view of impermanence, from a Buddhist standpoint too. We are all sentient beings in a constant state of flow and change, ignorant and deluded; we are also all *one* in the sense that every sentient being is originally a buddha. We're all the same, all one world. We can be enlightened by the very delusion that defines us. That delusion itself can be the source of our liberation.

If everything is changing, then we ourselves—with our egos—aren't permanent! But there is one pure thing that does not change, which Bohm describes as a kind of invisible ether from which everything arises and into which everything eventually evaporates. The Dharma calls this *emptiness*, which is uncreated. Mind and matter are not separate; they are different aspects of one whole and unbroken moment, in a constant state of flow.

In our life as we live it, an actual day is simply *one unbroken moment*. However, we tend to experience time as consisting of various divisions. We divide our day into one- or twelve- or twenty-four-hour periods. After a Dharma talk, for example, most of us expect to have lunch at noon, and later perhaps go for a two-hour hike. If we see everything as divided up in time, that's literally how our lives become. But in fact, all our lives are fundamentally a single thing. They are *one*. And this *one* is incomparable.

The way we divide time up can be alarming. That's why there's often apprehension as the New Year approaches. We blow horns and wish each other Happy New Year, but still we silently wonder if we're really ready for the unknown year to come. Some people facing this juncture turn to fortunetelling or astrology for answers.

But in a sense, really, you make a new year every time you come to any significant juncture of time. Perhaps you realize that you've been sitting for fifteen or twenty years and you feel that you're still far from *samadhi*, unwavering mind. When you investigate fully, however, you can see that all things are one, and that the perpetual motion of distraction is also calling you to return to your inherent nature. Perhaps you realize this suddenly, or perhaps it's been over years of practice. What you're feeling is the same as *not* being distracted. It's offering you a chance to go home, if you know where home is.

Little by little in your practice you discipline mind, body, and breath. Breath disciplines the mind, and mind disciplines the body. In that order. You need to practice regularly, and not miss an opportunity to establish a foundation through your practice. Otherwise you'll be homeless, like most people. But if you truly know where home is, you can be at home any time, any place, not divided and not separate.

In your everyday life, everything you do reflects the depth and strength of your sitting practice. And what is important in daily life is maintaining confidence. Say that at work you feel distraction surfacing, that you are coming to a certain juncture. If you go this way one thing will happen, and if you go that way something else will happen. Which will it be? Dharma discipline can help you make that choice. Will you be confident or not? Can you stand firmly behind what you're doing, whether it's resolving an argument, or making a left-hand turn in your car? Will you simply repeat your karmic conditions blindly, over and over? It's a matter of confidence, of intention. If you recognize the juncture, you can make the choice, reaffirm it, and be ready to confirm it again a hundred thousand times.

Make the choice! Even if you don't do anything, that in itself is still a choice! You always have choices. One diminishes you; another may strengthen you. What'll it be?

There was once a Zen master, Zuigan (Ch. Ruiyan Shiyan), who lived alone in his hermitage. To guard against becoming absent-minded during the course of the day, he would address himself by calling out:

"Zuigan?"

And then he would answer, "Yes!"

"Zuigan?"

"Yes!"

This is instructive. Even a Zen master accomplished in zazen kept calling his own name, reminding himself to be present. He was making the choice to be present, and then reaffirming it, again and again. Whatever it takes, you can always call yourself and make the choice to be present.

BUSSHO:
THE BUDDHA-NATURE

W

E PRACTICE IN a beautiful, tranquil, rural setting at Sonoma Mountain Zen Center, overlooking the Valley of the Moon. Sonoma Mountain is an ancient mountain, and is considered sacred by local Native American tribes, the Pomo and Miwok. One really feels a subtle, mystical quality in the pervasive quiet and stillness, especially on a cool, damp morning just before the fog has lifted.

In one of our chants the Dharma is described as "infinitely subtle." The Dharma goes beyond the conditioned self. We do not understand it intellectually, with the conceptual mind. We can't see it; we can't hear it; we can't really speak of it. It is not dependent on any particular conditioning, not on who we are conditioned to think we are. All we can do is *not* think about it—just receive it. This is subtlety in essence. Ordinarily we conceptualize with our minds; we judge with our opinions. Simply receiving something directly is transformative.

However, first we have to let go of the "I," the "mine," and "me."

The Dharma didn't just float down on a cloud to grace us. It came from Buddha himself, and through the profound efforts of each of our ancestors. We sit zazen, and may achieve *samadhi*, but to hold and see everything equally in our sitting *and* in the world involves an attitude quite different from the way most beings live. To see everything equally is the liberation of the Middle Way. It's a matter of regarding everything as having equal value: not as better or worse, but all of the same value. At this point we begin to be liberated from our attachments.

Traditionally, Buddhist teachings state that we all *have* buddha-nature. The Mahaparinirvana Sutra states: "All living beings, all have buddha-nature."

Many students assume that buddha-nature is something that one can get or attain: that is, they believe that by practicing zazen consistently, they'll eventually be graced by the Buddha and achieve their true nature. The paradigm "if I do this then I'll get that" may be what most of us live by, but it is conditional. Dogen questioned this interpretation for a long time; he finally determined it was dualistic and rejected it outright.

To counter the prevalent school of mainstream Buddhist thought, Dogen wrote "Bussho: The Buddha-Nature." In doing so he transformed the orthodox thinking of his time, essentially turning the meaning of buddha-nature on its head. To "have buddha-nature" is not the right statement, because it indicates subject and object. Dogen tells us that it is not something one can *have*; it just *is*.

For his ideological opponents, *bussho* was the "nature of Buddha," and was seen as some kind of divine grace finding its place in sentient beings. But this is conceptual; *bussho* used this way is merely a word. Dogen's *bussho* is neither the nature *of* Buddha, nor something *from* Buddha. Dogen saw that buddha-nature just *is* Buddha: the buddha-nature is the world *as it is*, right in front of us. In other words, everything we encounter is buddha-nature, beyond our likes or dislikes. Our lives are literally buddha-nature. To realize this is to see that whatever we encounter is the self. *This* and *that* are actually *one*, seen not as subject and object but as what is incomparable, beyond value—empty.

The Tathagata Buddha said, "All that there is without anything missing, 'there-is' is the buddha-nature. Tathagata abides forever. There-is and there-is-not alternate."

In reality there's no Zen and no Buddhadharma, because originally there is nothing. That is our first realization. In other words, what we call buddha-nature is only our life as it is, wherever we go. We can't escape it. As Dogen says, "It is the nature of the world, as it happens. There is a Buddha: it is the no-nature of things. And this no-nature is called emptiness."

One can say that there is nothing where everything comes from, because emptiness is exactly where everything *is*.

When we become distracted, or lose direction, it's easy to seek satisfaction in trifling things, as if we could maintain our lives exclusively by, say, going shopping. But material stuff won't bring happiness or joy.

With the ever-present social media platforms now—YouTube, Facebook, and so on—we live in greater delusion and distraction than ever, because of the entertainment and frequently distorted views of social media. Our ignorance—our delusion—in this materialistic world obscures our true nature. It seems almost as if there's a conspiracy against the spirit!

But, once in a while, perhaps you'll have a glimpse at sunset. At the exact moment the sun sets, you may see a green flash on the horizon. It's that vivid green, and then, flash—it's gone! You'll see. From time to time you will have a glimpse like this. You may see a flower, or you may smell something, or you may walk into a room and there's a certain atmosphere, and you recognize it is *it*. This is how you recognize your buddha-nature. It leaves an indelible impression. And then distractions enter. That's life. Possibly the darkest aspect of our world now is that the rapidly changing technology dominating our lives, with its constant distractions, obscures our true buddha-nature.

Dogen says, "All things Buddhists call karma are subject to the law of cause and effect." That is, the linking of cause and effect is the basis of karma. This means that we're all subject to the subtle relationship of dependent co-arising—and that deeply understanding this is the only way to understand cause and effect.

The Dharma of dependent co-arising teaches that when there is *this*, then there is *that*. When *this* appears, *that* also appears. When there isn't *this*, there isn't *that*. When there is no longer *this*, there is no longer *that*. This will make perfect sense when we understand that there is no *I* and no *mine*. Nature, arising, and co-arising are pure emptiness.

Everything appears from conditions. Conditions cause things to appear, and conditions cause things to disappear. So, if I say ego exists, then the objective world exists. This is one source of separation. If subject exists, then object exists. Conversely, if I understand that *I* cease to exist, then *object* doesn't exist. In other words, if the ego ceases to exist, then that objective world ceases to exist also. To put it another way, we don't have to depend on concepts—such as ego and *I*—for our existence.

This extinction of the ego occurs in meditation practice. In *shikantaza*, the conceptual *I* ceases to exist, while physically we're vibrantly alive, just sitting. When we practice *shikantaza*, we're not asleep; we're actively *illuminating*. There is vivid energy, clearing the mind. In *shikantaza*, the mind is resting in its source—emptiness.

Dependent co-arising essentially says that if *I* exist, *it* exists. "Dependent" in this context means mutually symbiotic in nature; "co-arising" means simultaneously. If *I* exist, *you* exist; if *you* exist, *I* exist. So when there's *this*, there is *that*. When *this* appears, *that* appears. When there isn't *this*, *I* no longer exists. When *I* no longer exists, *that* will no longer exist. In essence, there is no permanent *me* and *mine*. To have an ego is a big delusion; there's really no substantial ego to be found.

Where, actually, *is* your ego? Can anybody tell me? Can you show me?

Nagarjuna, the great Indian Buddhist philosopher of the second and third centuries—Zen's Fourteenth Ancestor—was the founder of the Madhyamaka school of Mahayana Buddhism. It was he who first refuted the common belief that buddha-nature is something we have or can get.

In "Bussho: The Buddha-Nature,"* Dogen described Nagarjuna preaching to the people of South India:

> Nagarjuna said, "If you want to see the buddha-nature, you must first of all forsake the I and the mine. . . . The buddha-nature is neither large, nor small, neither broad nor narrow. It offers no benefits, no rewards. It never dies; it is never born." Dogen added, "The ultimate eloquence spontaneously expresses itself without sound or color. The ultimate preaching has no fixed form. . . . Speaking about buddha-nature, one could say that it is no other than *enclosures, walls, tiles, and pebbles.*"

In other words, buddha-nature is all things that exist, as simple and mundane as they are. The Sixth Ancestor, Daikan Eno (Ch. Dajian Huineng), said, "Seeing the nature is being Buddha." The buddha-nature is simply seeing things as they are. Or *as it is.*

Zen engages in the present. Everyone has the potential to see everything *as it is.* But to see this, to realize it, you have to do a lot of emptying out, unraveling the conditioning that you have and that you are actually burdened by.

Your conditioning—your social culture, your traditions—none of this will help you to become happy; it's not clarifying the mind.

"There is" and "there is not" is the dichotomy that makes everyone suffer. There is, and there is not. You cannot get out of it. But in zazen

---

* Translation by Eido Shimano-roshi, paraphrased by Jakusho Kwong-roshi. —Ed.

practice you may be able to go *through* it. "There is" is no other than "there is not." They cancel each other. If they don't cancel each other then you're bound to suffer. And remember, it's not just what the Buddha said—it is the truth. Buddha's first noble truth was that life is suffering. Maybe you think that doesn't sound very positive; you want it to be more upbeat. But what he also meant was that life is impermanent. No one can refute that. If you don't have any insight on impermanence, then the conditions forever become your life and cause you suffering. Impermanence is the buddha-nature. Buddha-nature is impermanence. Impermanence is emptiness. Emptiness, impermanence, buddha-nature: it is aspatial. It is atemporal. You cannot grasp emptiness.

Dogen ends his whole essay on buddha-nature with these puzzling words: "Three heads and eight elbows." This refers to the monstrous form taken by Gozanze, a Buddhist wisdom deity, one of the Five Wisdom Kings of Buddhist lore. The name Gozanze means Conqueror of the Three Worlds—he triumphs over the worlds of desire, form, and no form. His two feet represent meditation and wisdom. His first two hands, representing the world of the buddhas and the world of the living, are sealed, forming a *fist of wrath*: the seal that liberates the world.... Thus, Dogen's whole discourse is an exhortation to wisdom, a fierce wisdom, like the wisdom of Gozanze. But note that the fist of wrath is for liberation, not for harming.

Symbolic figures like Gozanze all represent aspects deep within ourselves, which we can manifest in our everyday lives. They are not external. They are to remind us of aspects of our true nature. Just as Kanzeon (Skt. Avalokiteshvara) represents the aspect of compassion in us, Gozanze's fist of wrath embodies the fierce wisdom and courage we have within, as we vow to liberate all sentient beings—who are no other than ourselves. We don't have to say yes to everything anymore. Like Gozanze, we stand firm and we hold our ground.

And we're like Nagarjuna himself: he was sometimes referred to as a triumphant dragon, sometimes a ferocious dragon. Sometimes we have to be ferocious, to stand up and spring into action. Or stand up and stand still! But be steadfast!

There's a kind of warriorship behind all this: you have to have the courage and strength to go on, not to give up, in spite of everything you encounter. This is the kind of spirit you need to put into your work and into your life! Wake up to all things!

Tibetan Buddhist teaching tells us there are four faults that prevent us from realizing our buddha-nature. This may sound negative, but examine these four faults closely.

These four faults in our practice are: too close, too easy, too profound, and too wonderful.

Too close: We are trained not to be introspective, but to look away from ourselves. We are conditioned for years *not* to look into our deep selves: the eye can't see the eye. Our buddha-nature is too close to us for us to realize. But it wants us to.

Too easy: All we have to do in this entire meditation practice, in the entire practice of the Buddhadharma, is to rest in our pure awareness, which is already within us. The Dharma would have died a long time ago if it hadn't already existed. It's always with us.

Too profound: We have no idea at all how great the Dharma is, and that is because of our conditioned, narrow views. If we did know how great the Dharma is, we would seek it; we would pursue it. Even if we have just a glimpse of it, that's OK: as we seek it, as we practice it, more comes into view. Practice, awakening. Practice, awakening. Just like night and day: night inspires day; day inspires night. There's this total dynamic working—*zenki*—that we're living, when we realize our true buddha-nature.

Too wonderful: The immensity of this, and this, and *this*—BAM! BAM! BAM!—is ineffable. It is too great for our usual way of thinking. It is boundless—it has no beginning and no end.

UJI: THE QUICK OF TIME

Uji is the moment-by-moment living quick of time.
—KOSHO UCHIYAMA-ROSHI

ONE OF THE most challenging fascicles in the *Shobogenzo* is "Uji," often translated as "Being-Time"—but this is not "being" or "time" in the Western sense of the words. Dogen coined the term *uji* to express time in the context of the Buddhadharma. These brilliant insights are not understood by reading and analytical study alone; true understanding of Dogen's writing is experiential. I find Uchiyama's translation of *uji* expresses this best.

In "Uji," Dogen challenges our everyday notion—our usual, linear, twenty-four-hour experience of time. Dogen posits that time is not only "sometimes" but also, and above all, it is immediate, living time. "Uji" begins with a poem by Yakusan Igen. This paraphrased version is based on *Shobogenzo* "Uji" in Gudo Nishijima and Chodo Cross, trans., *Master Dogen's Shobogenzo, Book 1* (Dogen Sangha, 1994, 2006), 91.

WORDS OF THE ANCIENT BUDDHA

Sometimes standing on the top of the highest mountain . . .
being time

> Sometimes plunging down into the deepest ocean . . . being time
> Sometimes three heads and eight elbows . . . being time
> Sometimes eighteen feet or six feet high . . . being time
> Sometimes a monk's staff, a fly whisk . . . being time
> Sometimes a stone pillar or a lantern . . . being time
> Sometimes Mr. Smith or Mr. Jones . . . being time
> Sometimes the whole earth and the vast sky . . . being time

The words *sometimes* and *being-time* are translations of two possible readings of the original written characters. *Sometimes* at the beginning of each line indicates time passing, time coming and going. That's our conventional idea about time.

On the other hand, *being-time*, or *uji*, means that being and time are one and the same, that all phenomena are one time—that they exist at once—and the meaning is transformed. It's really wonderful to look at things and to experience our world in this way, because everything we do is at *just one time*. We're conditioned always to be thinking about the next thing. But right now—the time being—is *being* time, or being-time. It's a big relief to rest in the awareness of buddha-nature. It's always with us.

The highest peak and the deepest ocean, the good earth and the vast skies symbolize the entire universe. From the unimaginably vast, to the smallest, humblest of objects (such as the fly swatter), being-time covers the entire universe. Nothing is left out.

Three heads and eight elbows? What creature is this? It's that Wisdom King Gozanze again! A fighting spirit, protector of the Buddhadharma. He may look fearsome, but he represents the enormous strength and energy needed in this practice. This fighting spirit of Gozanze is not outside ourselves.

Eighteen feet high? That's the standing Buddha. Sitting Buddha is six feet high. So, while standing we are all about the height of a sitting Buddha!

Conventional time is linear: it goes one way, marked by the twenty-four hours of the day. This is time moving forward independently of us, like a train going from the past, through an instant of present, and on to an almost unknown future. But to think of time only this way is dualistic, separating us from the past, present, and future.

We normally divide up space or time—for example, by calculating time in increments of hours, night and day, and past-present-future; or by measuring space as the distance between two points.

We are confined in this way. But, after all, as Dogen said, "How far is the sky from the ground?" The open space of zazen is a continuum. In the spaciousness of *samadhi*, there is no this and that, or here and there. And this open space remains continuous, even when we don't always feel it; it's all one space, one present time.

In writing "Uji," Dogen wasn't speculating about what time or being could be; it was an account of what he knew time to be through his own practice.

"Uji" compels us to practice zazen right here, right now. It is zazen as *total combustion*—incinerating all our preconceived, conditioned ideas, and dropping off body and mind.

Instead of total combustion, we could use the word *ignition*—it's like turning on a car's engine. In lighting a candle, we ignite the wick. It illuminates. And it burns up! That's what we're doing in zazen. Spontaneous combustion, internal combustion, igniting—whatever the term, this combustion burns through and extinguishes the three delusions of greed, anger, and ignorance. Through entrusting ourselves to being-time, to our posture and breath, and not to our thinking mind, we create this combustion by breathing. In and out.

Combustion can occur in *kinhin*, walking meditation, as well. When doing *kinhin*, we take half a step. This is not just walking slowly. It *is* slow walking, but in this slow walking there is this combustion so that the "I" is no longer ego-I.

When I'm doing *kinhin*, I count. First step, on the exhalation, right foot: I count *one bosatsu**—that's ten seconds. Inhale, and then the left foot: *two bosatsu.* ... Inhale, then the right foot: *three bosatsu,* and so forth up to ten. Then we continue, beginning at one again. This is a way of concentrating fully on the breath.

We are counting, Buddha is counting, one to ten—but it's not belabored—over and over and over again until we've mastered the counting. We keep on counting until we're not counting. And then—it is spontaneous combustion, it's *zenki,* total dynamic working! We're totally alive! That's good *kinhin.* It is said that good *kinhin* does not move. It is stillness in motion. We're not going anywhere. We are completely present. This *kinhin,* walking meditation, is *uji.* Each of us is in the instant of the present moment.

In the Kannon Sutra for Prolonging Life, we chant:

> Morning mind is Kanzeon
> Evening mind is Kanzeon
> This very moment arises from mind
> This very moment
> not separate from mind

At "this very moment" we experience *uji*—being-time. Do you understand? We're not chanting *about* Kanzeon, or talking *about* Kanzeon. As we chant, it's with the compassion that's deepest within us.

Speaking of Kanzeon reminded me of an elderly Japanese monk named Takunin who used to visit Genjo-ji occasionally. He traveled alone, which was unusual for an elderly monk, and would just appear, unannounced. Once during *samu* (work period), Takunin was tackling some gardening tasks outside the zendo, and I gave him a pair of garden clippers. I assumed that he knew what he was doing, but he clipped off all

---

*Bosatsu is Japanese for "bodhisattva."—Ed.

the young tender shoots at the base of the tall ancient redwood tree. I held my tongue, remembering that one must not assume anything, especially when encountering someone with a pair of sharp clippers! Still, he did *samu* with true spirit.

I feel a little bit sad because I didn't really appreciate him when he was here. The last time I heard from him, he sent me a postcard with a picture of Kanzeon. On it he wrote, "This [Kanzeon] is your most intimate friend." At the time I thought, this is not my most intimate friend. But she is. Someday you too will feel the same way about Kanzeon.

KATTO:
INTERTWINING VINES

THIS MORNING when I walked into the zendo I saw the peonies on the altar, and their beauty astounded me. When you first see a flower, it is beautiful before you name it; it just *is*. It's at the instant even before the moment of the present.

These peonies come from the Buddha's garden here at Genjo-ji. A couple of years ago the head gardener uncovered some deeply buried bulbs when turning over the garden soil in late autumn. She replanted them, not knowing what kind of flower they would produce. The following spring new plants emerged and bloomed, to our delight—sensational pink blossoms. Since then, they have spread and produced abundant peony blossoms each spring. I think of the peony as our land lotus.

All along the fence enclosing our large garden, wisteria grows. We planted the vines when we first arrived here on Sonoma Mountain. Having grown for some forty years, the wisteria now completely shields the garden from the road, offering privacy. It has scarcely died back during the winter before buds spring forth again, and they are often in full bloom when we celebrate Buddha's birthday in April. Forming part of the flower shrine to the baby Buddha, the wisteria flowers celebrate the Buddha's birth too.

In our wisteria, there is a deeper significance. Wisteria is the symbol on our temple crest, drawn from the crest of Rinso-in, Suzuki-roshi's five-hundred-year-old temple in Japan. The meaning of the crest is found in Dogen's essay "Katto," the title of which is translated as "tangled, inter-twined vines," like kudzu or wisteria. Wisteria flowers are beautiful as they cascade down a wall, but the wisteria vines, like kudzu, are impen-etrably tangled.

There's a meaning behind the physical aspect of objects, just as we ourselves are more than objects or subjects. We experience this for our-selves in practice. The actual word *katto* means "kudzu." It has a nega-tive connotation because kudzu is a highly invasive perennial plant with climbing, entangled vines—a noxious weed for farmers. And, in general, we just don't like to see things all tangled up—entanglement upon entan-glement. This entanglement represents delusion. So the essay "Katto," meaning "a tangled vine of kudzu" (in our case, wisteria) is talking about spiritual entanglement—intertwined, delusional thoughts.

However, Dogen encourages us to use *katto* to cut off *katto*. Generally, we try to get rid of things that we don't want, to cut them out. But doing this just because we don't like something is not a good way to deal with it. To meet what we dislike head-on—to meet dislike with dislike and use it—is like fighting fire with fire. To cut off means to sever, but in Zen, when we cut, we don't cut in two—we cut in one. Do you under-stand? When we cut, it's still one.

Dogen says, "Generally sages study in order to cut off the root of their spiritual entanglement, but do not use their entanglement to cut off entanglement. Do they not know how to use entanglements to cut off entanglements? It is rare to find anyone who knows that entanglements cannot be separated from transmission of the Dharma."

Or, to put it another way, we use delusion to cut off delusion. Delusion cannot be separated from enlightenment.

Great enlightenment has no beginning and no end. On the other hand, delusion has no beginning and no end either. We cannot separate delusion from enlightenment—they are intertwined. This is the essence of the fundamental interrelationship of all things, which is emptiness. We can only enlighten delusion. Enlightenment and delusion are both always there, simultaneously. They coexist.

When I was a young student, I always wanted to get away from delusion. I didn't want to identify myself as a deluded person. But sure enough, that thought is itself a huge delusion!

You can play at Zen for a long time until at some point you realize that you're not playing—Zen is your whole life. From this point on you can practice wholeheartedly.

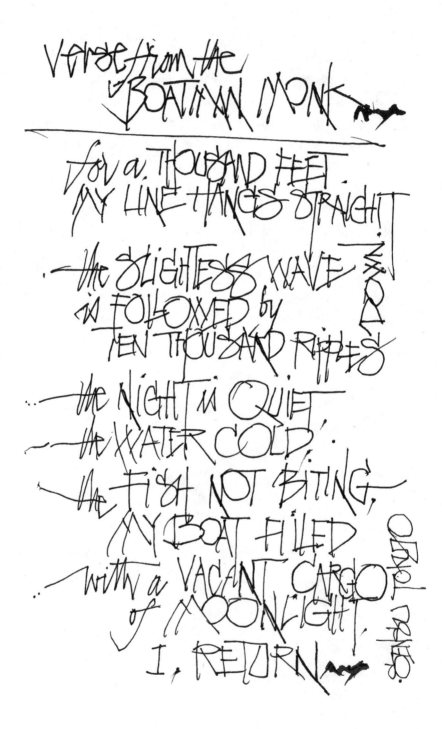

Verse from the
BOATMAN MONK

for a THOUSAND FEET
MY LINE HANGS STRAIGHT

the SLIGHTEST WAVE
is FOLLOWED by
TEN THOUSAND RIPPLES

the NIGHT is QUIET
the WATER COLD
the FISH NOT BITING,
MY BOAT FILLED
with a VACANT CARGO
of MOONLIGHT.
I, RETURN

TEN THOUSAND RIPPLES

ONE OF THE most beautiful chapters in the *Shobogenzo* is "Kai-in-Zanmai," the title of which translates to "Samadhi, the State Like the Sea." These are words of the Buddha, which appear frequently in the Flower Ornament Sutra and the Lotus Sutra—the sea being a frequent metaphor for the mind.

In this fascicle, Dogen wrote, "Because of not speaking of the appearance of self, myself is in the middle of the sea. The surface before me is eternal preaching, as ten thousand ripples following a single slight wave, and the surface behind me is the Lotus Sutra, as a single wave following ten thousand slight ripples."

"My self is in the middle of the sea" means that you are in the center of the universe, but not in an egotistical sense. Since you're in the center, you are relating to everything, before and behind and everywhere. Everything. "The surface *before me* is eternal preaching as ten thousand ripples following a single wave."

"Before me" is *zenmen*. Here, *zen* means "in front" and *men* means "face" or "surface." *Zenmen* means the actual scene before one's eyes. At the same time, it suggests the pivotal instant even *before* the moment of the present. I'm not talking about the present moment. I'm talking about the instant *before* the moment of the present. BAM!

This "before me" is very important. It means everything you behold is the universe. Actually, this is your realization of truth: whatever the eyes see is *it*. Nothing is hidden from you. Anything in front of you is seen, and that object is no longer an object. The idea of object is not there. And then—it is again, but perceived in a different way. And you return to yourself. Through that intimacy you see everything around you, as nothing is hidden—because you have given up your ingrained habits of greed, anger, and ignorance.

Through zazen practice you'll find intimacy with the relative and the absolute. There is no dichotomy, no contradiction. It's all one thing. This intimacy with all things becomes manifest. Isn't that wonderful?

Dogen's reference to "the Lotus Sutra, a single wave following ten thousand slight ripples," reminds me of this poem, written by Chinese Zen Master Sensu Tokujo (Ch. Chuanzi Decheng), a poet born four hundred years before Dogen:

TEN THOUSAND RIPPLES

For a thousand feet my line hangs straight down.
The slightest wave is followed by ten thousand ripples.
The night is quiet, the water cold, the fish not biting.
My boat filled with a vacant cargo of moonlight, I return.

Ten thousand ripples following one slight wave. Not a big crashing wave, just a small one. Many things happen subtly this way. If you're in a hurry, you will overlook ten thousand things—ten thousand ripples, ten thousand stars, ten thousand people—it can be anything. Dogen paraphrases the fisherman, saying, "Even though I have wound and cast a thousand feet or even ten thousand feet of fishing line, regrettably, the line just hangs straight down."

So you return to the surface before and the surface behind—those waves, Dogen's waves and ripples—but now it's the instant before and the instant after, *zenmen* again. "Before" and "after" suggest momentary occurrences of reality, flashing. BAM! BAM! They're happening right in front of you.

The fisherman notices the night is quiet. It's just like being in the meditation hall: it is quiet, and there's nowhere to go. The fish are not biting, but it's OK, because the fisherman realizes that though his boat has no fish, it has a vacant cargo of moonlight. And with that he returns. In returning, where does he go? He goes home.

That vacant cargo of moonlight is the emptiness of true realization.

Sitting in delusion

SITTING IN THE DARK

TWICE A YEAR at Genjo-ji we have a thirty-day intensive practice period called *ango*, which means "peaceful dwelling." This tradition dates to Buddha's time, when he and his followers would retreat from their travels and practice during the monsoon season. Traditional *ango* periods in Japanese monasteries last for a hundred days, but ours are only one month long. During *ango*, there are longer periods of zazen, beginning very early in the morning, sitting in the dark. The candle on the zendo altar is the only light. This allows us—in fact it obliges us—to look inward, making zazen before sunrise a moving experience.

Our thinking minds are created in two ways: we look either in or out. If we are always looking out, we start chasing ideas and projections from the moment we get up in the morning. Thoughts start accumulating; if we go on doing that, we may eventually create a small life filled with anxiety and fear. Meditation practice is basically a matter of looking inward, allowing all thoughts to become one.

Little by little, as we sit in the zendo, the darkness becomes light. Eventually the sun shines through the door, casting light on the dark redwood walls, the glowing hardwood floor, revealing a beautiful color of warmth.

During *ango* we take three small meals a day together. Since we eat in silence, we begin actually to taste the food and enjoy it for what it is and for what it brings forth in ourselves. These meals are served in the zendo in formal *oryoki* style, from which the Japanese tea ceremony originated. Sometimes the *tenzo*, the head cook, may serve lasagna, and though we might prefer to have a big plate and forks and knives, our lasagna serving is limited to one small black lacquer bowl. *Oryoki* means "just the right amount." Eating in *oryoki* means that we receive just the right amount of food.

In every activity during *ango*, we need to be aware of the right amount. Perhaps we can carry only one log of firewood, while the next person manages three, and someone else even more. We each need to understand our own right amount. This isn't a matter of better or worse, as the conditioned mind asserts. In Zen terms, everything in this zendo has equal value, or *toji*. This is discriminating awareness, *prajna* awareness. *Prajna* awareness means simply being fully, 100 percent present, open to receive. This doesn't take years of training. *Prajna* awareness is in everything we do, wherever we are.

I remember Suzuki-roshi serving us tea on his hands and knees during *ango* long ago. We were only twelve naive young students, but he believed in us and honored our true nature. Years later, in Poland, I served all sixty *sesshin* students tea this way, and I realized how still and calm it felt to be kneeling and offering wholeheartedly, fully present.

If you are serving an *oryoki* meal, you kneel, you pour, you serve. You give. The person before you receives an intimate gift. You'll find the ritual very moving, whether you're serving or receiving. It is so moving it may bring tears to your eyes. And you see clearly that we are all the same buddhas and sentient beings. Discrimination has no relevance.

When the head server carries the Buddha offering to the altar before a formal *oryoki* meal, we are venerating Buddha, so he is served first. When the *ino* says "Please pause" at the end of meal, we may still be cleaning our *oryoki* bowls, but being aware of the server entering the zendo, we stop at that moment to restore our buddha-nature—not thinking, just sitting here. That is practice. That's what we do. Put the bowl down and just sit there. That's all.

Ango is led by a senior student called the *shuso*. At the end of the retreat, there is a dramatic closing ceremony in which students are urged to challenge the *shuso* by asking questions in *mondo*, or "Dharma combat." This is the opportunity for everyone to step forward in real debate! Each student has a different question, and may continue to question the *shuso* until satisfied with their reply. *Mondo* encounters can be utterly serious or wildly humorous. Anything goes, but there's always great depth of feeling.

One literally becomes the question one asks.

It may be called combat, but the *mondo* invariably turns out to be a win-win situation, since it occurs in a Dharma context. No one is concerned with who asks the best question or receives the best answer, and everyone wins. At the end, when the exchanges are over, it's as if the questions have been answered by *shuso* and students together, each rising to the moment and engaging with the other, each ascending to the way of Dharma.

The formal words the abbot says before and after the *mondo* resemble a traditional address to Buddha's great assembly. He addresses everyone as "Dragons and Elephants." In Asia the dragon is a symbol of realization, holding the bright jewel within its jaws. And elephants, sturdy and steadfast, show a deep constancy as they move majestically across plains and forests. Just so, in Zen we can realize ourselves in each activity by practicing steadfastly with constancy and awareness.

FEAR

Fear, you have no origin.

I N ZEN, facing fear—fear of your own existence, of suffering, sadness, and pain, even your hesitation—this is all good! Understanding this is what being wholehearted means. Even if your wholeheartedness lasts for a single second, it remains a great possibility. This is the proclamation of the lion's roar.

Fearlessness—the understanding that you need have no fear—is what zazen is about. It all depends on your level of concentration in zazen. You need to recognize that sometimes you are successful, totally concentrating, and sometimes not. You mustn't be too hard on yourself, scolding: "There I go again . . . got caught up in my thoughts again. I won't do it next time." There will be many next times, but you must continue to stick with zazen.

An example of ungrounded fear is an experience I once had during *ango,* one of the month-long practice periods here at Genjo-ji.

There's an evening practice called fire watch during summer *ango.* The *shuso* (head student) is assigned to do fire watch, which takes place after the last period of evening zazen. Holding two wooden clappers called *kaishaku,* they bow to the zendo altar, and then exit to circumambulate the temple grounds, striking the clappers every eight steps. This is a signal for everyone to put out all fires and lights and prepare for sleep. The sound of the clappers needs to be audible to the entire sangha.

One part of the walk, where the path narrows and goes through a densely wooded area, is very dark, even with a full moon. Some students told me that they felt a sense of primitive panic going through that spot. One student shuddered and said they felt the presence of Bigfoot there! Then my turn came for fire watch. As I reached the dark wood, I too felt a rush of fear. Something or someone might have been lurking behind me. Suddenly I recalled something I'd read years before—*Fear, you have no origin!*—and poof! the feeling of fear just dissolved. I also knew that if I'd been in real danger, my original, primordial nature would have told me to flee.

That fear I had in the woods is a *thought* of fear, which creates the feeling. In practicing meditation, we study the nature of a thought and what's behind it. It was *prajna* awareness that told me "fear, you have no origin." It's a matter of seeing through the thought of fear. Behind the thought there is nothing! This nothing is not the usual nothing that we think of; it is the spaciousness of emptiness.

If a situation is actually dangerous, your *prajna* awareness will warn you to go another way. This isn't a psychological ploy. Zazen itself arouses *prajna* awareness, which is the way to meet fear directly. Again, observe what's behind the feeling of fear, which is the *thought* of fear, and ask yourself, what's the nature of that? That's really the study. Even if there's nothing behind such a moment, that "nothing" can also be everything: great massive mountains, foaming waves of clouds in the sky.

SONOMA MOUNTAIN KOAN

ZAZEN AIMS at turning the mind away from thinking, to know that in the pure present in which we're sitting we don't need to think. We turn away from any thought, whether good or bad, in order to return to the mind itself, where all thoughts originate.

The related question of where the mind source comes from, however, is one that human beings rarely ask themselves. But since what we call mind can't be grasped as an object in itself, the very act of trying to focus on it—that is, seeking an objectless focus—has a particular effect. In turning back from any preoccupation with the mind itself, you're shining your awareness directly on your mind source, which is something ungraspable. This may sound strange, but when you focus on where your thoughts come from, they'll naturally diminish because you're no longer entertaining thoughts at all. They are only fabrications. This focus, this awareness, is called *eko hensho*, turning the light inward and illuminating the self.

Koan practice is another technique of meditation that aims at turning the mind away from its conditioned logical thinking. A koan is not a riddle or a trick question. It posits an idea or situation or image that cannot be understood conceptually. It must be turned on its head, upside down, or over, or backward, before one can even begin to realize it.

It's questionable whether Dogen stressed koan practice to the same extent as Rinzai masters with their graded system, which involved passing koans continuously. In his early teachings, Dogen seemed to play down the value of koan methods. Nonetheless, prior to the *Shobogenzo*, he had devoted an entire book to three hundred koans.

Dogen's successor, Ejo, remarked that we may understand only one out of a hundred or a thousand koans, but what is most important is that the understanding arises out of our wholehearted sitting. This expresses Dogen's attitude as well.

You deal with koans not with your analytical thinking mind, but with the strength of your zazen mind—Big Mind.

Koans take many forms. In fact, my first koan had to do with my early experience of zazen. I hadn't been raised in a tradition of cross-legged sitting, and found the lotus position very painful. But eventually I realized that if the posture were practiced over and over again, my body and mind would get used to it. My response, both physical and mental, changed completely. In *shikantaza*, just sitting, I "got" the answer to my koan.

Shikantaza is a koan. Not a verbal koan—the sitting itself is the koan.

It's well known that in Rinzai Zen, pressure is put on students during meditation to answer or illustrate a koan. You might be given a question like "What is the sound of one hand clapping?" You'll see your teacher about it two or four times a day, in formal *dokusan*. As you go to the interview room, the teacher might listen to your footsteps. If they hear that you're going too slowly or quickly, they'll sense that your mind is straying as you walk, and ring the closing bell before you even open the door. Sorry, maybe next time!

Any valid response to a koan will come as a result of continuous effort in sitting zazen, just sitting. That is literally what *shikantaza* means. The pressure of koan practice is intense, and there's a kind of spiritual materialism that can arise here. The practice may become competitive, as when comparing notes with other students—for example, asking "How many did you pass?" Such egotism can surface anywhere, though, in any religious practice.

I've heard of great Zen masters whose own teachers had held them to just one koan, and never let them pass and continue to the next. So, it's not a matter of how many you answer. There may be a few thousand more . . .

When I was a young Zen student, I was afraid to meet fierce Rinzai Zen masters who used koan methods in their teaching. That fear of intimidation can be a sign of stress, but at the same time it's good to feel it, because it makes you super-focused and alert. It's an adrenaline spike.

What is the sound of one hand clapping?

This famous koan was written by Hakuin in the eighteenth century. I must tell you a story about Genjo-ji's contemporary version of this koan.

When we first began to build Genjo-ji on Sonoma Mountain, of course we had applied for a building permit. We soon received a letter from the Sonoma County building department supervisor, warning that there might be litigation when we began construction, because the permissible noise level could not be above the sound of one hand clapping!

Reading this, I burst out laughing. What a reply to get, straight from Sonoma County offices! We are connected! A week later I received a letter from another county official, wanting to know what the sound of one hand clapping was, and I realized how many others were considering the same question. Even our lawyer, who'd been working with the county, asked about it one day. The fact that so many people were interested meant that they actually did hear the sound!

Suzuki-roshi explained Hakuin's koan by saying that usually we think that clapping with one hand makes no sound, but one hand *is* sound, even though you don't hear it. There is always sound. If you clap with two hands you can hear it, but if sound had not already existed before you clapped, you couldn't hear it if you tried.

Listen!

There it is! There's sound before you hear it.

Sound is everywhere, Suzuki-roshi pointed out. But don't try to listen for it. If you try, your ears will not hear it. If you don't try to listen, the sound is everywhere. Can you hear it? Only when you *try* to hear is there no sound.

It's everywhere. Do you understand? You can laugh, but there is already sound everywhere, always.

SUFFERING AND PAIN

ZAZEN PRACTICE is a discipline of breath, mind, and body, training you to become less caught by duality such as "this is good, this is bad"; "this is delusion, this is enlightenment"; or "this is dark, this is light." Such dichotomies cause suffering.

It is important to know that in Zen you're not trying to get rid of anything. In Western culture, you think that when you cut something, you always cut it in two: keep one piece and throw the other away—but in Zen you just cut in one. It's always one. It's not two. Two is where the suffering starts. Do you understand what I'm trying to say? You cut in one. You don't throw anything away. In fact, you *can't* throw anything away. It just becomes something else!

Following his great enlightenment, the Buddha proclaimed the four noble truths. This proclamation was the foundation of Buddha's teachings, transmitted nearly three thousand years ago.

The first noble truth is that there is suffering, and the cause of suffering is impermanence. There is nothing permanent in our lives, nothing to hold on to.

Much as we try to hang on, to cling and to desire more and more, everything in our lives will eventually vanish. Impermanence creates conflict and suffering for us. And we see this in the world all around us as well.

Does technology cause suffering? We've become so dependent on technology, rather than on our own inherent wisdom that, little by little, technology has taken over our lives. Of course, this is advantageous in many ways—for example, in photography, going first from film to digital cameras, and then to smartphones. You can take hundreds of pictures at a fast pace. Before, you could only take one picture at a time, and the film was only so long, and it took time to develop. But now, when photography is automatic, can it be art? And who is taking the picture? Technology has no wisdom or compassion, no ceremony, no ritual. Just speed.

How do you put wisdom and compassion in an app?

How does technology cause suffering? It depends on how much you use it—and how you are used *by* it. Much of the time you're being used by it. You know the game—there will always be a newer, smarter smartphone. Then there will be another, newer one, and then another one. And you'll want that—that's the whole game. You'll want that one and that one and that one. It's endless.

To return to the four noble truths, the second truth is that there is a cause for suffering: it is caused by our inexhaustible desires. This is purely scientific, logical. It's karma, the law of cause and effect.

Desires are inexhaustible. Because we are driven by wants and desires we are never satisfied. The point is, in this wealthy country, how can we actually find satisfaction? The Dharma shows us the way.

In war-torn countries, where people have experienced severe violence and deprivation and are impoverished, they can still be happy. One student here went to Greece to help refugees fleeing from Syria. She says that people there can still smile and laugh. Perhaps there's a sense of joy because things are so dire in Syria that they feel happy just to get to Greece. They don't know where they'll be tomorrow, or what their existence will be. But they can still feel joy. Many people in poorer nations have that innate joy too, despite their lives of great deprivation.

The third noble truth is the cessation of suffering. When you feel pain you can't help it, because you have a human body—but suffering may be optional. During zazen, there's no need for anger or blame. And you don't have to anticipate pain before it actually occurs. You just accept the pain. You accept the pain as it happens, and it hurts like hell, but at the same time you don't have to anticipate the next round. Then, when the pain stops, oh, joy! Relief! And then, again, the pain returns. But suffering is optional. Pain is unavoidable, so you'd better just relax and enjoy it. Or *be in* pain.

The fourth noble truth is that there is a way to end suffering: the eightfold path. This is Buddha's insight and his seminal teaching, and it is beyond religion. It is a way of life. Buddha's proclamation may have been the most profound teaching ever, but it is one of the most neglected doctrines in history. Not many people listen, or understand, or really investigate these truths. Who are we? Where are we going? Wherever we live, whether we're rich or poor, we are all subject to suffering and pain and fear. And the fourth noble truth proclaims an end to suffering through mindful living—that is, the eightfold path: right view, right intention or resolve, right speech, right action or conduct, right livelihood, right effort, right mindfulness or "bare attention," and right concentration or samadhi.

When you're young, when your mind is most likely open, you're in a particularly good place to study Zen. You have the beginner's open mind. Suzuki-roshi remained in America to teach because he saw that we, his students, had this spirit of open-mindedness. We hadn't yet had much life experience, and we were receptive to doing something new—including sitting zazen!

For myself, sitting cross-legged was difficult at first. I experienced a lot of pain. But, you know, there are two kinds of pain. You have to make that distinction. One kind of pain comes from injury. The other kind will just gnaw at you in every position you move to; you cannot alleviate it. How do we distinguish which kind of pain it is? The one that will hurt because it's *aaaarghhh*—that's the one that may really harm you. This pain that you experience is the one that hurts physically, so you can just move slightly, adjusting your position. OK? So *that* pain issue is settled.

But the other kind of pain—the one that keeps on gnawing at you— that's the one you work with. You breathe. You breathe in and you exhale with the pain. Exhalation is the most important part of your breath. Your exhalation comes from down here, the *tanden*, the power point of the body. You must know that this is your primordial point of energy. Its strength depends on your physical condition and your mental state. When the mental waves become calm, the pain also calms down. In fact, the pain sometimes vanishes.

Students in a week-long *sesshin* endure seven days of this. Imagine, seven days of doing nothing. It takes you to your edge. You're testing yourself. You're finding out what your capacity for pain is.

Sitting zazen this intensely, you'll find out your inherent tolerance and stamina. Zen practice is really preparation for whatever difficulties you may encounter in your everyday life. Zen *is* life. Your whole life.

ZEN STITCHING

Each stitch is like the earth exploding.

L ONG AGO, when Buddha and his cousin Ananda were traveling on foot, they realized they didn't have any way to distinguish themselves from other spiritual groups in the area. So, as they were walking along through fields of rice paddies, it occurred to them to make robes with a pattern like the rows of rice paddies. They used only discarded cloth to make their robes—even cloth that had been used to wrap corpses. They washed the cloth many times in the river, dyed it with saffron, and cut it into pieces. These pieces, squares and rectangles in the shape of rice paddies, were then sewn together. One shape represents enlightenment and the other represents delusion. This reminds us of the teaching that delusion and enlightenment coexist—they are literally sewn together.

The Buddha's robe has been made this way ever since. In certain lineages, the primary practice is sewing. Monks and nuns sew as an expression of their zazen, and the garments are still painstakingly made by hand.

The ordained Zen priest's robe is called the *okesa*, or *nyoho-e*. We wear our robes over the left shoulder, just as monks did nearly twenty-six hundred years ago in India. It takes one hundred and fifty hours to sew one *nyoho-e* by hand.

The *rakusu*, the bib-like garment worn by Zen practitioners who have received Jukai, or lay ordination, is a shorter version of the *okesa*, and takes thirty to forty hours to sew. Like the robe, the *rakusu* represents the Buddha's teachings and the vows one has made. Wearing the *okesa* or *rakusu*, one is actually wearing the Buddha's robe and his teaching. Before donning them in the morning, one chants:

> Limitless is the robe of liberation
> A formless field of benefaction
> Wearing the Tathagata's teaching
> Saving all sentient beings.

In preparation for Jukai, students sew their own *rakusus*. This sewing is a practice in itself. Each time a student pierces the cloth with the needle, they say, "I take refuge in Buddha."

The needle is pointed toward the person who is sewing. The stitch is not a forward stitch, but a backward step stitch, which moves the seam forward. This sewing leaves a visible mark of the mind's activity: when the practitioner is truly focused, each stitch is like a spark.

It requires complete attention. At first glance, the sewn lines of the *rakusu* may look perfectly straight; but sometimes when one turns it over to see the back—"Ahh, there it is, that zigzagging, that's where I missed! That's where my mind was distracted."

This practice was transmitted to us by Eshun Yoshida-roshi, abbess of Kaizen-ji temple in Japan and Dharma heir of Hashimoto-roshi. At Katagiri-roshi's suggestion, Suzuki-roshi invited her to come to America to teach the sewing practice at San Francisco Zen Center. Though never given full credit for the transmission of the robe to the West, Eshun Yoshida-roshi was the first teacher to bring this *nyoho-e* practice to America. Before she died, Yoshida-roshi taught the Dharma of sewing to Katagiri-roshi's wife, Tomoe-sensei, with whom I studied.

It's a difficult practice. My own experience with sewing had been very negative, as I'd always associated this activity with being poor. When I was a child, we didn't have much money and my mother had to make many of the clothes for a family with five children. So, in my own *rakusu* sewing, I had to work with a feeling of shame. I made a lot of mistakes in the beginning. At one point, while I was sewing, I realized I'd sewn my *rakusu* onto my pants! I was too embarrassed to show anybody!

Because of my resistance, I had to take the complete class twice with Tomoe before I finished my *rakusu*. However, the time I spent sewing turned out to be quite a wonderful experience, as I silently repeated, "I take refuge in Buddha" with each stitch.

In the silence of sewing I could hear the needle drawing the thread through the cloth, and that hearing is in itself a practice. To this day, I remember clearly the sounds of Tomoe's needle piercing the fabric, the pins dropping into a little cup. Through those sounds I sensed the purity of the practice, and my heart was deeply touched. This is the practice of Zen.

Here's a little story.

> Tozan's (Ch. Dongshan Liangjie) Dharma brother, Shenshan, was sewing.
>
> Tozan asked, "What are you doing?"
>
> "I'm sewing. Can't you see?" Shenshan huffed.
>
> "What is sewing?" Tozan asked.
>
> "Each stitch follows each stitch," Shenshan said.
>
> Tozan responded, "If my companion of twenty years says so, I guess there's a point. Let him drown in his dullness."
>
> "Well, what would *you* say, elder?" Shenshan wondered.
>
> "Each stitch is like the earth exploding," Tozan replied.

That is true *samu*. When I sewed my pants to my *rakusu*, maybe that was an explosion too, calling me to pay attention!

JUKAI

Jukai is the ceremony in which Zen students receive the Buddhist precepts, or vows; it is also known as taking refuge. It is lay ordination, a confirmation of one's deep commitment to the three treasures of Buddhism. We take refuge in the three treasures: Buddha, Dharma, and Sangha.

Many young Americans take refuge like, oh, it's a piece of cake—just a nice ceremony! Taking vows in Zen Jukai goes much deeper. The Buddha is the essence of your life, the light within yourself. The Dharma is Buddha's teachings. The Sangha is the community of people who practice together. We are all practicing in our lives, individually and collectively, and this Sangha really includes the sun, the moon, the stars, and the trees as well. It's all Sangha. Everything is one. Everything is sacred.

The best way to practice with constancy is in a sangha, where we are all practicing together. In receiving the precepts, you are making a public statement to the sangha, openly asserting before all of us that you're no longer narrowly preoccupied or clinging to your small self. Constantly attending to that small self has no real benefit. In asserting big self, you're helping others emerge from their own darkness, because they are also you. Big self is beyond the duality of self and other.

Suzuki-roshi always said he gave precepts to students so that we could help others. All sentient beings need help. If you help spontaneously and wholeheartedly, it actually helps you as well. When I travel to Poland and Iceland every year to help students in Europe, I am deeply moved by their commitment and resolve, and return energized.

With Jukai, formally accepting precepts, your demeanor will change. Receiving the precepts doesn't mean that principles—such as don't kill, don't lie, don't blame others—are imposed on you from outside. Zen Buddhist precepts are developed through profound personal realization.

In Zen stories, there are people who were suddenly enlightened simply by hearing their names called. We tend to take such encounters casually. But in Jukai, when you formally receive your Dharma name, will you hear it? Will you be truly present to receive it? In Jukai, you are making a public statement—you are deliberately turning away from greed, anger, and ignorance, and committing yourself to turn toward the awakened mind, toward Dharma truth that frees you from samsara.

If your name is called, will you really hear it?

SHIHO:
TRANSMISSION CEREMONY

I WAS ORDAINED AS a novice monk by Shunryu Suzuki-roshi in 1970. I would spend only one more year with my teacher before he died, practicing calligraphy with him. I felt completely unprepared and unconfident, but I went through with my ordination because I believed in my teacher; I believed in the way he lived, and in what he wanted to transmit. The whole ordination process touched my heart most profoundly.

I had been studying closely with Suzuki-roshi and learning the practice of kanji in Japanese calligraphy, in preparation for Dharma transmission. However, Roshi became very ill with liver cancer and died before he could complete the transmission with me. After his death there was considerable confusion at San Francisco Zen Center, and I encountered many delays. Eventually I asked Hoitsu Suzuki, Shunryu Suzuki-roshi's son, to complete my transmission. In fact, Hoitsu had been his father's choice to transmit the Dharma to me, so in the end Suzuki-roshi's wish was fulfilled.

In the years following Suzuki-roshi's death, I continued to study the transmission ceremony intensively under Kobun Chino Otogawa-roshi.

I drove down to Los Altos every week for five years to study with him. I was fortunate to have the support of other Zen teachers as well. One was Maezumi-roshi, the founding abbot of the Zen Center of Los Angeles, who occasionally came up to San Francisco to teach.

At one point early on, Maezumi-roshi invited me to visit him at the Los Angeles Zen Center. While we were having tea in his room, he went into his closet and brought out a calligraphy scroll, saying simply, "This is for you." On the back of the calligraphy he had written the translation in pencil: "You must pass through the gate."

I had a studio by our house on Sonoma Mountain, and I hung the calligraphy scroll up over the altar there. One night, after several years, the scroll suddenly fell off the wall. There was no logical reason for it to have fallen. When it fell from the nail, it did not touch anything on the altar below. It just fell directly to the floor. When I woke up the next morning and found it lying on the floor I thought, "Wow! I have to tell this to Otogawa-roshi!" When I told him, his response was, "Oh, hmmmm . . . Well, who are you going to do the transmission ceremony with?" Just like that. He suggested a number of teachers to choose from.

When the time came, I chose Hoitsu Suzuki.

The trip to Japan for my transmission ceremony in February 1978 was a daunting experience, as it was the first time I had ever been to Japan. My family and I were to stay at Rinso-in, Suzuki-roshi's original temple, where Hoitsu Suzuki-roshi was now abbot and lived with his family. At the San Francisco airport, the Japanese flight attendants all bowed to us in unison. As they bowed repeatedly, I thought to myself, I'm *really* going to a foreign country! Even with my Zen training, I realized Japan would be utterly strange to me. The formality and discipline in Japan are things that we may not understand in our Western culture. However, the formal discipline in Zen is practice. It is both preparation and realization.

It was wintertime, and the five-hundred-year-old temple was very cold. There were very few warm places. One was the *ofuro*—the deep communal hot bath used in the evening. There was an old lady attendant who stoked the fire and helped take care of the temple. In an American bath we just sit in our grime, but in Japan one showers first, and then goes into the *ofuro*. I was really grateful for that *ofuro* warmth. Another warm place was the kitchen, of course. But most unusual was the warmth of a light bulb placed under a table, with the covering tablecloth forming a curtain to contain the heat.

Hakusan Noiri-roshi, a highly regarded Soto Zen teacher in Japan and an authority in the Shiho ceremony, had just refused to take any more Western students. He said he couldn't count on them; they didn't commit themselves, but tended to drop out, not keeping their vows. But fortunately, he agreed to officiate in the ceremony for me.

When we visited Noiri-roshi's temple, I was struck by his towering stature. I told him I wanted Hoitsu Suzuki-roshi to give transmission on his father's behalf, but he looked at Hoitsu and said, "Can you sign

Jakusho Kwong and Hoitsu Suzuki at SMZC

the name of a dead man?" Right away I knew Noiri-roshi was a great teacher! He came to Rinso-in temple to officiate the ceremony, which was performed in the traditional manner.

I hope we never lose the traditional ways, as they connect us to our ancestors.

The day of the ceremony began with everyone—monks, wives, and children—cleaning the temple for the whole day. This *samu* was really the beginning of the ceremony. When Noiri-roshi's car arrived later that afternoon, the wind was blowing very hard and blew everyone's robes up. The wind! It was Suzuki-roshi's spirit presence—he manifests himself in the form of wind. His energy, his force, visits us at key times, at ceremonies and remembrances. He was entirely present then.

Inside the temple, I waited at the altar. The door opened and Noiri-roshi strode in, robes flying. The first thing he said was, "Oh, very cold. Rinso-in very cold. *Good* practice place!" It was a truly auspicious time.

Suzuki-roshi had passed away before he could complete taking me through all the steps of the transmission ceremony. Writing three particular documents in kanji was one of the final steps. I was to practice this now at Rinso-in with Hoitsu Suzuki-roshi, under Noiri-roshi's direction. A special plum rice paper, not readily available and used only for this purpose, had to be ordered. I was to write the names of all the Buddhas, and the full lineage chart of our ancestors, in kanji calligraphy on this paper. There was also a *shisho*, the official document necessary to verify my Dharma transmission as successor to Hoitsu Suzuki-roshi. After that, these three documents had to be stamped with Dogen's seal as well as other stamps of acknowledgment.

I was given only one sheet of this plum rice paper for each document— no room for error! But it was so cold in the room and my hands were shaking so much that I ended up making a mistake. Noiri-roshi, overseeing the proceedings very strictly, was cross with me. Nonetheless, he happened to have one extra sheet of paper so that I could complete all three calligraphies, but he admonished me severely, saying, "You cannot make a mistake now!"

I think this kind of strict training is absolutely necessary. If one resists, transmission won't occur. As one writes the kanji names of the ancestors of our lineage, the whole past, present, and future are right here. It's not easy, but transmission comes in this way.

Hoitsu Suzuki-roshi and I represent the ninetieth and ninety-first generation after Shakyamuni Buddha, and are fortunate to be part of this lineage. The lineage is our true family.

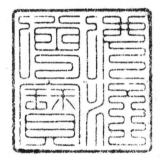

Eihei Dogen's seal

THE SPIRIT OF PRACTICE

THERE WAS a warm familial spirit at Rinso-in temple when I stayed there for my transmission ceremony, and that spirit remains alive today. Now my son, Nyoze, visits with his wife and son, just as I did then, when Nyoze himself was a small boy. To us, the spirit at Rinso-in epitomizes true Zen spirit. As we receive it, we maintain it as we bring it to Sonoma Mountain Zen Center.

How do you bring forth and maintain this kind of spirit in your own practice, in your own everyday life? This is very important. You sit over and over and over, and do *sesshin* over and over, and it may become automatic; your practice can become a dead form, and you drift away. But Zen spirit is the most important thing to keep alive. How to ignite your mudra? How to ignite your *gassho*? How to give it life? When you give it life it gives you life. It transcends space and time. You have to have spirit, the *spirit of practice*. Some people have it from the beginning. Actually, we all have it; we just need to bring it forth.

Zen spirit—what is it, Zen spirit, anyway? How do you carry yourself? I saw one person walking during *samu* (work period), slouching along with his hands in his pockets. I said to myself, "Oh, that's not good"—

because in this habitual posture he was absent-mindedly maintaining the familiar comfort of his conditioned world.

Can you maintain Zen spirit, this awareness, in all your actions? I just saw a student, in the middle of *ango sesshin*, walk up to the windows of the sangha house in the morning and carelessly yank up the delicate window shades, really hard. Where was her awareness? Practice in everything you do.

Zen may be one of the only spiritual disciplines to emphasize so strongly that all activities be done with deep awareness. Zen in cooking, Zen in the arts, Zen in athletics, Zen in daily work—whatever you do, wherever you are, is practice. Pay attention. Feel the hammer in your hand before striking the nail. That is *prajna* awareness. Work practice—*samu*—is no other than life itself.

When chanting, some people just mouth the words, moving their lips—but the chant is not coming from the *tanden*. When it actually starts coming from the *tanden*, the chanting is burning off past karma and future karma. The chanting manifests that you're here 100 percent. That is what the practice is—to be where you are 100 percent. That's Zen spirit.

In training, I watch how students bow. If you bow weakly, just going through the motions, that's not bowing. When you truly bow, you are surrendering to the Dharma, submitting to the Buddha within yourself.

In ordinary encounters, no one wants to yield, but in Zen you learn that you cannot receive until you yield. It's in all your bows: prostrations, *gasshos* to one another, bows to Buddha, bows to yourself.

Zen is both spiritual practice and philosophy. In the philosophical sense, Zen is not the metaphysics that you're taught in the West. Ontological metaphysics emphasizes the nature of being, the nature of existence—but that's about existence, or truth, in the sense of conditioned, conceptual reality.

In the spiritual sense, Zen is simple and direct. It is experiential, leading the practitioner to a direct experience of reality. The religious traditions that promise something are offering an idea, an artificial concept. Zen is nonconceptual; it does not promise anything.

Certainly you need to study—not only in zazen—and to read closely. There's so much Buddhist literature it's mind-boggling. Through study you get inspiration—but you've got to study *and* practice. One ignites the other. This is combustion. It is *zenki*—total dynamic working.

Dogen says: "Therefore, cease from practice based on intellectual understanding, pursuing words and following after speech, and learn the backward step that turns your light inward to illuminate your true self." This is *eko hensho*.

In Zen, understanding doesn't mean intellectual understanding. It is knowing, through and through. Knowing *truly* is found in practice. It's not that practice gets to realization or truth—practice and truth are one. When you truly practice you awaken; you awaken to the truth, to the ultimate truth. What is it that you practice?

You practice letting go of this self—this conditioned self. And when you can let go of this self, forget this self, you are one with what you're doing. That's where your realization comes; realization of the ultimate truth that's behind everything. It sounds pretty simple, but it means practicing continuously, sitting over and over. So if you are to study, you have to *really* study, and you have to practice with spirit.

And what about *now?* BAM!

Maybe you're at a low ebb. When you're feeling down and dispirited, do you begin doubting yourself, and have no confidence? That doubt is negative, destructive. That's one kind of doubt. But there's another kind of doubt, which is simply questioning. Questioning, but not in a negative sense. Wondering. This is Great Doubt.

Your ego wants you to think that practice follows a direct course, but it doesn't. Practice does not go in a straight horizontal line. That would be flatlining! Your practice goes up and down, up and down, and you go with it. You go along with life—the life surrounding you: not just your life but universal life, the life that includes the rocks, the trees, the thousands of trees, the sky, the earth—the omnipresent life. In this universal life we are mutually dependent. Interdependent.

Once I asked a student here if he practiced what I taught him, and he said, "Yeah, I tried. But it didn't work." You really have to practice with constancy—regularly, whole-heartedly. Sit zazen. One hundred thousand times!

Some practitioners will realize the truth and some will not. Even if you practice ten, twenty, thirty years sitting, some of you will "get it," some will not. That's just being truthful. Other religions preach that if you adhere to a certain belief you are guaranteed to go to heaven or attain nirvana. But it's not true. Some will, some will not.

So, my question to you is, how important is practice in your life?

THE NATURE OF RITUAL

It is not about memorizing, but about experiencing
and realizing our pure presence.
It is stillness in motion; a flowing stream moving without thought.

RITUAL IS OFTEN defined as a solemn ceremony, a series of formal actions performed according to a prescribed order. The common idea of ritual is that it's just ceremonial religious stuff. But in Zen, it's not just ceremonial stuff. Zen rituals are forms that guide us toward realizing our buddha-nature.

Zen includes many rituals that take many different forms in practice. For example, *kyudo*, the martial art of archery, is a continuous ritual—preparing to release just one arrow, in slow motion. The first time I watched *kyudo*, I said to myself, just shoot the arrow! Just shoot it! But the archer is not interested in the actual shot. As she goes slowly from movement to movement, each movement . . . *is* the shot. Concentration, posture, and movement are more important than actually hitting the target. When she is finally ready to shoot, she takes the archer's stance and places an arrow in the bow, slowly raising it with the feather fletching pointing to her gut. If the archer loses her balance, the arrow may pierce her gut. She is fully engaged; the attention does not wander. That arrow reminds her to be right here, right now. The arrow is guiding the archer as much as the archer guides the arrow.

Here's another sort of guide: in the parking lot at Genjo-ji there are railroad ties to guide drivers, indicating the boundaries of the parking area. If you had come up here before we had those ties in place, how would you have known where to park? Someone once drove his car all the way up to the steps of the zendo! Why? Because there was no guide.

Zen rituals are a different kind of guide: to be *right here*, fully present. That's the essence of ritual in Zen.

One example of ritual is our practice of offering bows during the morning service. Suzuki-roshi introduced us to the practice of nine bows—nine full prostrations. This is unusual. In Japanese monasteries and temples, it's generally three bows. But when Suzuki-roshi encountered his egocentric young American students, he took one look at us and decided we should bow nine times. At Sonoma Mountain Zen Center, we still maintain this ritual.

Americans are usually so intent on maintaining the self, the ego. So, in the ritual of bowing, we surrender ourselves. Even a simple *gassho* is a gesture of surrender. A *gassho*, pressing palms together with a bow from the waist, is a universal gesture that expresses basic human goodness. It's a symbol of respect, of honoring the other, and of giving ourselves.

When one gives something to somebody, it mustn't be given while inhaling; that signifies holding back. It is natural to exhale when giving something. Just so, when we bow, we bow on the exhalation; it's spontaneous. We are *giving* on the exhalation. As we put left and right palms together in *gassho*, we are putting subject and object together. We put all dualities together, bringing them together now in the bow. Delusion and enlightenment are one. As we bow in full prostration, we give, surrendering ego. We return to our true selves. There is no thinking at this point. Rising to stand, we inhale, renewing energy, and we return to the world in serenity.

There are six aspects of ritual in Zen Buddhist ceremonies, eliciting strong responses in the participants. These correspond to the five physical senses plus mind.

The aspect of *sight* is simply the deep awareness of what is right in front of us, noticing everything vividly, just *as it is*.

Sound is manifested in the striking of the *bonsho*, the great temple bell. When it is struck properly, the *bonsho* vibrates, and the sound continues, reverberating deeply. When we experience this, when we really hear it, the vibrations of sound cut through our thinking. That's sound, the subtle force of sound.

Smell is incense. Suzuki-roshi used to say that offering incense is a message to Buddha. The incense we use in the zendo is from Tendo Nyojo's temple in China.

Taste takes physical form in the offerings of tea, sweet cakes, and perhaps fruit.

Touch in Soto Zen ritual is represented by water. In ancient times water was considered sacred. Now we just turn on a faucet, and unthinkingly let the water go down the drain. But water is sacred, as we are again realizing on this endangered earth.

The sacred water I use in ceremonies here at the Zen Center comes from Mount Kailash in Tibet. One of my senior students, Chuck Tensan Ramey, was trekking in Tibet and made the arduous pilgrimage to Mount Kailash. En route he stopped at the sacred Lake Manasarovar. He drew water from the lake and brought it back to Genjo-ji in an unbreakable Nalgene bottle sealed with duct tape. This is the water I use to this day in formal ceremonies such as Jukai.

The last aspect in ritual is *mind*—purification of the mind, for which I chant a mantra before most ceremonies. This mantra purifies the mind, the water, and the whole environment as well, producing good karma. It is mind protection.

Every day you unconsciously perform little rituals, whether you are religious or not. Every day you get up in the morning and brush your teeth. Even that is a ritual. How do you brush your teeth? Do you brush just to be done quickly, so you can eat breakfast? Do you brush so your teeth are thoroughly clean and bright? Look at each activity. Pay attention. And enjoy brushing your teeth! Look at this small ritual as part of caring for yourself, instead of a dull routine.

It took me a long time to fully appreciate the beauty of ritual in Soto Zen tradition. It is not about memorizing, but about experiencing and realizing our pure presence. It is stillness in motion; a flowing stream moving without thought.

TOUCHING THE WATER

THERE IS an old Buddhist story about a group of Buddha's disciples, twenty or thirty of them. They went together to bathe at a large communal bath. As they entered the bath and waded into the water, they actually *touched* the water.

Spreading their hands, these monks (or nuns) really touched the water. As they touched the water, the water touched them. And because of its wondrous touch, their realization was actualized. They became realized disciples for that moment.

That was not the end of it, of course, because if one has had one realization, that's already in the past. Those monks had to continue to practice, day after day. Life is realization after realization.

Do you ever touch the water when you bathe? When you wash the dishes?

Does anyone touch water these days? The water touches us, but we just *use* water. We use it, we gulp it down, we consume it the way we consume everything. But—*touching* the water, you know . . . have you ever *really* touched water? I'll bet you haven't truly touched it since you were a baby!

Legend has it that at Shakyamuni Buddha's birth, a gentle shower of rain fell on the baby Buddha—only on him.

In a discourse given to commemorate Buddha's birthday,* the great Chinese Master Wanshi said, "Not receiving any sensation [in *samadhi*] is called right receiving. If you practice like this, each drop of water falls on exactly the same spot."

That spot is no other than you. In *samadhi*, you are in a state to receive the true Dharma.

In the same talk, Wanshi said, "When the pure water of the emptiness of self-nature and the radiant body of the Dharma realm are only faintly distinguished, then this person is born. Without cleansing the dusts from the body, because of this water's wonderful touch, he expresses clear realization."

Wanshi is referring to Buddha himself, reborn in his enlightenment. But he also points to us—without washing away delusions, we can realize our buddha-nature, glimpse pure *dharmakaya*, and experience realization.

Dogen commented on Wanshi's statement, asking, "How should [we] speak of the true meaning of [Buddha's] birthday? Dropping off the body within the ten thousand forms, naturally he had the conditions for this birth. In the single color after transforming the body, he saw the vital path afresh. What is the true meaning of our bathing the [baby] Buddha?"

Dogen answered his own question, saying, "Holding together our own broken wooden ladle, we pour water on [the baby Buddha's] head to bathe the body of the Tathāgata." This is the essence of Buddha's birthday.

Each year in April, we reenact the occasion of Buddha's birthday with an open ceremony here at Sonoma Mountain Zen Center.

We celebrate the historical Buddha's birthday, and the return of

---

*Taigen Dan Leighton and Shohaku Okumura, trans., *Dōgen's Extensive Record: A Translation of the Eihei Kōroku* (Somerville, MA: Wisdom Publications, 2010), 237.

spring—but it is really a celebration of rebirth and liberation for all of us. It is a very joyful occasion.

In the morning, a special sweet tea is prepared. A shrine of fresh flowers is set in front of the altar. The zendo is filled with more flowers, and crowded with sangha members, friends, and children of all ages. During the ceremony we proceed in turn to the altar, bow, offer incense, and ladle sweet tea over a small statue of the baby Buddha, who stands in the flower shrine in a shallow bowl of tea.

As we pour tea on the baby Buddha's head, we are bathing the body of the Tathagata—not just symbolically, but actually here in the zendo, in this living shrine. And in doing so, we are cleansing ourselves as well, because we are all baby buddhas.

Wanshi's observation, "Because of this water's wonderful touch he expresses clear realization," means that you can experience realization with something as slight as one drop of rain falling on your head. Or by an action as ordinary as touching the water when you wash the dishes.

If you have a clear realization, you are part of everything—the trees, the stones, the grass—and of everybody. And everything is you.

PAUL DISCOE'S TEAHOUSE
AND WABI-SABI

When moving a stone, one should first ask its permission. ⋮

ONE DAY long ago a young Paul Discoe—who would later take the Dharma name Zengyu and is now a master builder in traditional Japanese joinery—rode into Tassajara Mountain Zen Center on a motorcycle and ended up staying for years. Eventually, Suzuki-roshi sent him to Japan to study joinery construction, the ancient carpentry of building without nails. He apprenticed with a master craftsman who was one of Japan's living national treasures. His apprenticeship was long and tedious, requiring the sort of effort most young people don't want to make anymore.

He wrote me that he spent the entire first year of his training just planing wood. At last, one cold December day, he noticed that the shavings he was making were so thin that they rose into the air, and were impossible to distinguish from the snowflakes starting to fall. As I read Paul's letter, his description of the convergence of effort, tool, wood shavings, and falling snowflakes made a deep impression that touched my heart. We all have moments like this, deeply imprinted on us.

Here in California, Paul Zengyu recently completed the construction of a teahouse in the classical Katsura style, an elegant expression of *shibui*, of unobtrusive and subtle beauty. The details in this teahouse all express the characteristics of *wabi-sabi*, a certain Japanese aesthetic that Suzuki-roshi describes as "the simplest and most humble form and style of beauty."

Wabi-sabi describes a quality so direct that our experience is not influenced by anything else. Objects are profound in their simplicity. There is no garnishing. Imperfections are an important aspect of *wabi-sabi*. Beauty in *wabi-sabi*, conveying a sense of imperfection and impermanence, expresses the texture of emptiness.

In Paul's teahouse, the finely planed wood retains its natural finish; it is not oiled. The shingles on the roof are all hand-cut. All the textures and shapes convey a sense of *wabi-sabi* that enters your heart.

Paul's teahouse is beautifully landscaped as well, in keeping with the same spare aesthetic. The Japanese style of landscaping involves placing water and stones in an order so random that it seems to be from nature itself. This sense of something uncreated deeply touches the experiencing self.

In landscaping the teahouse, Paul chose two large stones of muted colors from the Yuba River and hauled them to the site. In addition, the stone for a nearby bridge and wall was shipped from China. All the stones were cut by hand and then placed according to a plan drawn freestyle. A particular kind of mindset is required to set the stones so that they seem random. If you consciously *try* to place stones randomly, your habitual thinking will make the effort difficult and contrived. Paul said that this was the most difficult part of the entire project.

A long time ago at Tassajara, Suzuki-roshi once directed his students to move all the large stones in the bed of the creek next to his cabin. It was quite a big project. And after this *samu* was finished no one could tell the difference, or discern the subtle change.

In the strict sense, *wabi-sabi* points to a reality that does not belong to any category of subjectivity or objectivity, whether simple or fancy—a reality that in fact makes both subjective and objective observation possible, so that everything comes to our heart. In the realm of *wabi-sabi*, we can see the whole universe even in a single drop of dew on a blade of grass. We see warmth and beauty in an ancient wooden door with cracked and faded paint. In contrast, normally when we catch sight of something irregular or imperfect, our first reaction may be rational analysis, rejection, or even emotional disturbance. The tendency in Western thought is to reorganize everything conceptually in our thinking mind, to manipulate the data of our sensory world, rather than to accept them as we experience them directly.

In the world of *wabi-sabi* there's no attainment whatsoever, no striving for perfection, no organizing mind. The existence of each object or design appears as the fruit of self-training and pure, direct experience. Once the savor of these fruits enters our hearts, confirmation of reality takes place. We see the beauty of flowers even as they are falling and are decayed. As this kind of pure experience is repeated, we develop a calm and deep understanding of—and deliverance from—life. We become like traveling monks, who fully appreciate everything in the world and nonetheless remain completely free from it.

Wabi-sabi is Zen made visible.

BODHIDHARMA'S TRANSMISSION

BODHIDHARMA WAS the first Zen master to transmit the Dharma of "just sitting" to China. He traveled by boat from India, a journey that took three years in those days. Then, heading north, he crossed the Yangtze River and continued on foot all the way to northeastern China, until he reached Shaolin. There he found a cave where he meditated for nine years. Finally, nearing the end of his life, he decided it was time to transmit the Dharma to his four senior disciples. He gathered them together, saying that the time had come for them to reveal to him what they'd realized. One by one they were to go before Bodhidharma to show their state of mind, their practice, their wisdom.*

Do-fu, the first disciple, said, "This is my view: Neither be attached nor detached to words or letters."

Bodhidharma immediately said, "You've got my skin."

The second disciple, So-ji, said, "This is my understanding: After

---

*The following paraphrased account is based on Shobogenzo "Katto" in Gudo Nishijima and Chodo Cross, trans., Master Dogen's Shobogenzo, Book 3 (Dogen Sangha, 1997, 2006), 31.

Ananda saw the Buddha-field of Akshobhya, he never looked back again."

Bodhidharma said, "You've got my flesh."

The third disciple, Doi-ku, said, "The four elements are originally bare. The five skandhas are not existence. In my view, there is not one thing to be got."

Bodhidharma said, "You've got my bones."

Then the senior disciple, Taiso Eka (Ch. Dazu Huike), rose slowly from his seat and walked up to Bodhidharma. He made three prostrations and then stood. He said nothing. He did not turn his back to Bodhidharma as he returned to his seat. He *was* zazen. Zazen sitting, zazen standing, zazen walking, zazen bowing.

Bodhidharma said to him, "You've got my marrow."

Bodhidharma eventually transmitted the Dharma to Eka, who became his successor, the Second Ancestor in Chinese Chan Buddhism and the Twenty-Ninth Ancestor following Shakyamuni Buddha.

When I first heard that story over forty years ago, I thought that Eka had the best answer. I was convinced that I needed to get the marrow. I thought that the marrow must be the best, and I didn't want anything less. But I was wrong. It was my mind thinking, "This is the best and that's the worst." That's just conditioned mind thinking, needing to be competitive, to be "better than." Actually, all four disciples were valued equally. You can't separate bone from marrow—it's not about outer or inner, best or worst. You are you, completely, and I am I.

According to legend, Bodhidharma lived to the age of one hundred and twenty. After his death, word came that he had been seen in the Himalayas walking home to India with one shoe hanging from his staff. When his casket was opened, his body wasn't there; there remained only one shoe. Hakuin pointed out that alluding to Bodhidharma being seen later, returning to India with just one shoe, was a way of expressing loss.

Loss is important in Zen practice. Usually people try to avoid it at all costs. But with long training and many hours of sitting practice, you surrender the self by working with loss. This is actually good, since every human being alive will experience loss.

Zen training will help you actively participate in loss. You don't invite it; you simply acknowledge it. Think of it this way: when you're on a train, watching the scenery from the window, you don't fear loss as the scenery speeds past and is lost to view. You realize that the train stays on the track and you stay on the train, even without that landscape. This awareness is the eye of Zen—this is active participation in loss.

You must lose, or surrender, something to be here. What do you lose? You forget about yourself, let go of your ideas about yourself. When you surrender your conditioned self, you're not spacing out; you become vividly present.

Losing is usually seen as negative, but in Zen it's part of all life. We've been so conditioned that the thought of not losing keeps us in a box. That grasping, holding on tight, is *duhkha*—suffering. And that keeps us from the happiness and joy of living this life. So just let go.

THE ONE GREAT MATTER

WHEN DEATH COMES, it pulls the rug right out from under you. What we thought was our world is not so, now.

In our culture, no one wants to confront death, but it is inevitable. Chögyam Trungpa Rinpoche once said that we don't have to worry about death because everyone is successful at it!

At whatever age we die, each death will be a unique death, depending on how we live our lives—or, how our lives live us. It's what we do with our mind and our body that matters: how we discipline and train ourselves, and become courageous enough to face all the fears we have buried inside.

Suzuki-roshi, when he had cancer, yelled at us in the zendo, "Death is the greatest teacher!" Death may be a moment of realization, if one has had a strong practice.

His Holiness Dilgo Khyentse Rinpoche, one of the greatest Tibetan lamas of the twentieth century and the Dalai Lama's root teacher, once remarked that the difference between Americans and the rest of the world is that we are so rich that wealth has become our disease. He also pointed out that we are too busy; we're so very busy, busy, busy, that we forget to ask: What is the most important thing? *What is the great matter?*

What is it? It is the matter of life and death. They go together, like light and dark. We all want to look toward the light side, but the light side includes the dark. Just think of the two faces of the moon. It is dualistic thinking to consider the two as separate.

Duality creates suffering—all the suffering that people want to ignore. But when it comes to witnessing death, there is no duality. It is always near; no one knows how long we will live. We have to wake up and live fully aware.

We fear death because we don't want to look at it. This basically starts with the fear of looking into our selves. But it's too late to look at death when we're about to die. Zazen practice is about dying while we're alive. Each time we sit zazen, thoughts come. Just let them go; don't grasp, and don't get attached to them. We're not judging them as good or bad. That thought? It's just a thought. Let it go. It's already dead.

According to the Buddhadharma, the self does not exist. There's no substance to ego. If ego did exist, you could come and bring it to me right now. Show me! In fact, even though *self* doesn't really exist, most of the world thrives on this delusion, the notion that this ego-self, driven by greed and desire, is real.

In our practice we swim against the stream. We don't have to be consumed by greed and dissatisfaction, by material desires—although I have to admit that even I, when I go to Costco, have the urge to buy stuff! This temptation is part of a setup, of course. The whole consumer market is directed toward our inexhaustible desires, our dissatisfaction, our suffering. It's not reality. But to go into Costco and buy just a bunch of bananas and nothing else, and then walk out—now, *that's* something! Because our intention is clear. We know what we need, and we know how to be satisfied.

With zazen practice, you'll become truly satisfied with your life. With discipline, you can experience true reality. And after that, then you return to the ordinary "real world" again. I hesitate to use that phrase. Your family says, "Oh, you're going back up there on retreat again, that's not the real world!"

But it *is* the real world. It's all the real world, whether you're staying at a Zen center, or away at school, or still living with your parents.

Zen practice may not take away all suffering, but it will lessen your burden. Zazen is a practice of nonduality. Duality makes you suffer, caught in the duality of good/bad, long/short, black/white. But when opposing thoughts appear in your mind while you're sitting—in the meditation hall, at home, or anywhere—you can allow them to appear, and let them disappear. If they arise, they can also disappear, because they were created. But there is something that has not been created, that's underneath it all. And that something is the one and pure clear thing. It is the unborn.

Shunryu Suzuki-roshi had a close friend, a Shinto priest who was also an artist. After Suzuki-roshi died in 1971, the Shinto priest made friends with Suzuki-roshi's son, Hoitsu. They became good friends with each other, even though usually Shinto and Zen priests don't mingle.

This artist-priest made beautiful oil paintings that were hung at Rinso-in temple. He would then ask Hoitsu to write a calligraphy of a poem for the painting, to convey its meaning. This was a tradition at the temple; I don't know if it is done anymore. Hoitsu said it was harder to use his own words than to write a quote from someone else's poetry.

When his friend died in 1978, Hoitsu held the funeral ceremony. As I was in Japan at the time, I suggested that maybe I could go with Hoitsu to assist him. I was still an inexperienced priest then, and didn't realize that I would be a burden to him. Young priests often burden their teachers because they want to help and to look after them. But this can be overwhelming, and Hoitsu just said no to me.

It was difficult for Hoitsu to write a poem for his friend on that occasion. After the funeral, he said to me, "Because I officiated at the ceremony, I had no time to cry myself." This is very important.

It is so important to express our grief and loss right away. Right now.

A TRUE FRIEND

Oskar Ingelsson was one of my senior students in Iceland. He was a pillar of Natthagi Zen Center, the Icelandic sangha in Reykjavik that I founded in 1986.

After many years of practice, Oskar died suddenly from a massive stroke. An unexpected and sudden death is a great shock for the living. Natural deaths from the illnesses of old age, like heart failure or pneumonia, are easier to accept. These natural deaths of old age are our friends, actually, because in time they teach us about life.

In the year before he died, Oskar expressed to me that he felt a strong calling to become an ordained Zen monk. In retrospect, I wonder if he sensed that he was going to die soon.

Oskar was the first person in the Icelandic Zen sangha to be ordained. His Dharma name was Dai-an Tenshin—Great Ease, Sky Mind. He had begun studying at Sonoma Mountain Zen Center in the late 1980s, soon received Jukai, and was then ordained as a priest. He became the first president of the Icelandic Zen Center, now officially named Natthagi Zen Center. Under his direction the sangha grew, and Zen Buddhism became an officially recognized religion in Iceland.

Some people are like bright comets. They come into our world. They live joyfully. And suddenly they're gone. Well, some people may not be bright comets . . . you never know. Each pot comes out of the kiln differently. No two are the same.

Oskar was just such a bright comet, though he was a very unassuming person. I didn't realize until after his death that he was an accomplished classical clarinetist. He studied under the first clarinetist of the London Philharmonic Orchestra, and graduated from the Royal College of Music in London. He then returned to Iceland to join the Iceland Symphony Orchestra, where he became first clarinetist. Eventually he found that working there was unpleasant. The other members of the orchestra were highly competitive; it was a culture full of envy, petty jealousy, and gossip—so he quit. He just dropped out of the orchestra and became a householder, staying home to take care of his two young sons.

He was subsequently hired by the National Radio Company of Iceland to manage a department of twenty employees, all women, recording music for radio. He soon realized that no one in the department knew or cared anything about music. He had a deep, heartfelt understanding of music, both how it was played and how it should be recorded, so he faced an untenable situation. He presented me with his dilemma: these employees didn't care what they were doing; they were there just to collect a paycheck.

I told him to fire them all! But, of course, he couldn't just do that outright. Instead, he retrained the whole department. He began by identifying the employees' problems and complaints, and empathized with them. He worked side by side with each one and developed close working relationships with all of them. They just loved him for what he did. And they all came to his funeral.

Over five hundred people attended Oskar's funeral and it was standing room only. I didn't know what would happen when introducing this Zen ceremony to Icelandic people who were not familiar with Zen Buddhism. Really, no one knew what the ceremony was about except the people performing it. But all went well. There was such a warm feeling throughout this celebration of Oskar's life, reflecting his own warm-hearted, funny, convivial nature. In my eulogy I urged the congregation, in the spirit of this fragile life, to actualize the qualities that Oscar expressed: strength, courage, vision, and joy in life itself. These are the marks of a spiritual warrior.

Although zazen practice is all about active participation in loss, it is still sad to lose someone we love. But when we lose a true dear friend like Oskar, he will always remain a part of our lives. We honor cherished friends by keeping them alive in our hearts. I will always remember Oskar's lively spirit. He returns to the ocean of emptiness, looking up into the vast spacious sky.

Oskar was the embodiment of the three minds: magnanimous mind, parental mind, and joyful mind.

Here is one anecdote about our close friendship. I always enjoyed visiting Oskar and his family when I was in Iceland. He was a very good cook, and he also made the best cup of coffee I ever had. He had a wonderful old coffee machine that made just one cup of coffee at a time.

After over twenty years of drinking excellent coffee with him, I had an idea. I thought that maybe I could have his coffee maker. Isn't it awful that I would have such a greedy idea? Nonetheless I approached Oskar—after we had a cup of coffee of course—and asked, "Why don't you give me the coffee machine?"

Oskar paused to consider, then said, "I think I'll have to ask my wife." Indignant at my suggestion, she came out and shouted "NO!" Later, when I went back to visit Oscar's family after his death, I told them I wouldn't take the coffee machine after all—it deserved to stay at home in Iceland—and everyone was relieved.

A poem from the late Korean Zen Master Seung Sahn:

THE HUMAN ROUTE*

Coming empty-handed, going empty-handed—that is human.
When you are born, where do you come from?
When you die, where do you go?
Life is like a floating cloud which appears.
Death is like a floating cloud which disappears.
The floating cloud itself originally does not exist.
Life and death, coming and going, are also like that.
But there is one thing which always remains clear.
It is pure and clear, not depending on life and death.

Then what is the one pure and clear thing?

*From https://kwanumzen.org/resources-collection/2017/9/15/the-human-route.

THE KOREAN MALA:
ON DANA

NEARLY FORTY YEARS ago, the Korean Zen master Seung Sahn, also known by the title Dae Soen Sa Nim ("Great Zen Master"), invited me to go to Korea on a pilgrimage with him. This was my first trip to mainland Asia. While we were there, he gave me my first Korean *mala* as a present, and his generous gesture made me very happy. A mala is a string of small beads used in Buddhist meditation. But this *mala* was enormous! Koreans are brawny, robust, extroverted people, and I think their *malas* resemble them. The *malas* have big beads, like a baby's toy: wooden beads strung on a wire ring. As you use the Korean *mala*, you hear *click—click—click—click*. It's a constant sound.

Three years later, I went with Dae Soen Sa Nim on the same pilgrimage, to a different temple. He came up to me saying, "I'd like to give you this *mala*." I blurted out, "I already have one. You forgot? In just three years?" Right away—there was my conditioned mind reacting! He looked at me and said, "Take it. Why don't you take it? Why don't you stop your thinking mind? Just take it." So that was a great teaching for me. We react and assume things so quickly just because of our conditioning!

Jakusho Kwong with Seung Sahn and Taizan Maezumi, visiting
Seokguram Temple in Korea

Nine years later, there was another pilgrimage at another temple. And
again, Dae Soen Sa Nim gave me another *mala*. This time, he pulled it
back and then proffered it again—a gesture that made it clear this was
an act of giving and receiving. I took it, gratefully. Ever since then, at the
beginning of each *ango*, or practice period, I have given this *mala* to the
shuso (head student) to hold. It provides them with energy, stability, and
focus while carrying it throughout *ango*. You can tell where the *shuso* is
by that steady *click—click—click* sound.

It is difficult for people to receive something. Just to receive. As you
receive, of course you are giving as well. In fact, you *have* to give in order
to receive.

Seung Sahn and Jakusho Kwong sitting in a yurt in California

There's an old story about heaven and hell. You're invited to a banquet with all sorts of delicious foods, prepared by the finest chefs in the world. But as you're about to eat, you realize that your chopsticks are so long that you can't get any food into your mouth! This is more than frustrating, if you're very hungry. This is hell!

The next night you're at the same banquet table again, with the same exquisite food, and the same chopsticks; however, this time you realize that when you pick up the food, you can reach far enough to feed the person across the table from you. And immediately, that person spontaneously feeds you in return. Here is the difference between heaven and hell. The table is the same, but your response has changed. This is *dana*, true generosity.

PAST TIME BECOMES PRESENT: CHÖGYAM TRUNGPA RINPOCHE

IT WAS ALLEN GINSBERG who first introduced me to Chögyam Trungpa Rinpoche, at Green Gulch Farm Zen Center in Marin County. There was no dialogue; I was a young monk, and I just bowed to him reverently. I came to think of him as resembling Kukai, the legendary Shingon master who walked from one end of Japan to the other, meeting many on the Way. Like him, Trungpa Rinpoche would also encounter many people, traveling from east to west in America. That's how he found Suzuki-roshi at Tassajara—an encounter, Trungpa Rinpoche said, that was "like looking at the burning tip of an incense stick."

Chögyam Trungpa Rinpoche was one of the first Vajrayana masters to appear at the San Francisco Zen Center. I can still see him talking with Suzuki-roshi in the courtyard—two teachers connecting with unforgettable presence, openly and completely there. Their relationship was so close that when one of his sons was born, Trungpa Rinpoche asked Suzuki-roshi to bless him. When Roshi touched the ceremonial wet willow leaf to the baby's head, the baby cried waaaah! At that same moment Roshi and Rinpoche simultanously shouted "BUDDHA!" It was a beautiful if startling response, and it showed how deeply the Dharma penetrated their mind and body.

Being in Trungpa Rinpoche's presence was always quite scary for me. But after Suzuki-roshi died, I found him very supportive. In many ways he was like a father. Whenever he was involved in an event in the Bay Area, he'd invite me and insist I sit in the first seat. This was a great honor; it meant I'd be the first to greet and introduce Rinpoche, but I was so shy I never knew what to say. I spent a good deal of time squirming in my seat. Once when he asked how I was, I answered inaudibly, "Fine." He responded with a vigorous "What?" making me feel as if in seconds he'd crushed me to pieces, and let the fragments fall gently into his palm. But I realized then that there was another, immensely generous aspect to his teaching and character—like when I innocently asked him about the *vajra* he was holding. Without hesitation he just handed it over to me, a gift. That's how it came to be on our altar.

I once heard a conversation between Trungpa Rinpoche and Maezumi-roshi. Maezumi-roshi began by saying, "I have nothing"—on the surface, manifestly untrue—to which Trungpa responded, "I have everything"—equally misleading!

After that, they both laughed and laughed. There was something wonderful in that exchange, beyond the underlying allusion to form and formlessness. They shared a spark, an inner liveliness. That's what Trungpa, Suzuki, and Maezumi were conveying to us.

Our responsibility is to wake up to this spark. As bodhisattvas we need to share this awakening with the entire world—especially when the world is experiencing so much suffering and loss.

I think what drew Trungpa Rinpoche to Zen was exactly what was conveyed in his conversation with Maezumi-roshi—that Zen is oriented toward "nothing," while Tibetan Buddhism responds to "everything." Trungpa Rinpoche seemed to have realized that the flamboyance of the Tibetan tradition, its tendency toward luxuriant elaboration of the stages of consciousness, needed to be balanced by Zen's deliberate austerity. While Tibetan Buddhism moves outward to a vast range of experience and feeling, Zen posits a kind of spiritual minimalism, or asceticism, even while participating in the world.

Trungpa Rinpoche was drawn to each of these living lineages: one with a clearly mapped path, the other with virtually no path at all, but both arriving at emptiness, the source of wisdom and compassion.

Fundamentally, what Zen and Tibetan Buddhism, especially the Kagyu lineage, truly share is their emphasis on sitting meditation. The late Kobun Chino Otogawa-roshi, who was invited to teach at Naropa University, represented Zen in the largely Tibetan environment there; he demonstrated that upright sitting meditation is what anchors both traditions. Kobun Chino and Trungpa were like Dharma brothers.

Chögyam Trungpa had a close connection with many teachers in Japan, especially those of the Shinto tradition. Before building Naropa Institute (now Naropa University), he invited a Shinto priest to come and bring the Dharma to the mountain. The Shinto priest came five years in a row. After the fifth year he said he didn't need to come anymore, because the Dharma was here already. Actually, this was an instance of *upaya*—Rinpoche's skillful way of introducing the Dharma to the West. But the West should know that the Dharma was already here. It is everywhere.

Trungpa Rinpoche gave teachings in many ways—and not only in his provocative and sometimes explosive Dharma talks. I remember forty years ago watching him sit for a long time in a big chair, with a glass of something on a little table beside him, while everyone waited for him to present a Dharma talk. After a while he picked up the glass and drank from it. Then he smoked a cigarette and put it out, as if he weren't even conscious that we were there. I don't recall the talk, but his movements, these wordless actions, were a teaching in themselves. I know now that it was a silent transmission.

Back in 1974, before Naropa was accredited, Trungpa Rinpoche invited me to Red Feathers Lake in Colorado to teach at Rocky Mountain Dharma Center (now Shambhala Mountain Center), and to bring my whole family. On the way, I wanted to follow the nearby rushing river to its source. There we discovered a rock face with tiny drops of water trickling down from a hidden spring. They were to become the life force of the river itself. Later, when we pulled into the parking lot of the future Shambhala Mountain Dharma Center, a seminar was in progress.

The next morning, my oldest son, Ryokan, who liked to fish, invited Rinpoche's twelve-year-old son, Sakyong, to fish with us. Rinpoche's attendants told us there were no rods at the center, but we had ours, and Rinpoche was accommodating, so off we went to Poudre Canyon. We caught a great many rainbow trout on that warm, beautiful day—at one point, amazingly, I even had three on one line! After a while, however, I noticed that Sakyong was holding a bent stick with no line. He confessed that his father had told him not to fish, and afterward we learned that Rinpoche himself had handed the fishing poles over to the neighboring Girl Scout camp.

Tibetans eat the meat only of larger creatures, thereby killing fewer beings and feeding many more. That evening we cleaned, cooked, and ate our catch. But years later I learned that, without saying a word to each other, no one in our family had ever fished again after that.

Rinpoche and I talked often that week, our exchanges mostly short and often delivered through example and demonstration. One evening, when I said during a conversation that something must be "the myth of freedom," I was startled to see him staring at me, eyes wide, glasses sliding down his nose. I had unknowingly pronounced the title of his next book!

We continued to meet that week and remained close long after that visit.

Much later on, just before leaving Naropa for Halifax, Nova Scotia, Trungpa Rinpoche told me that he wanted to come to Genjo-ji to visit Suzuki-roshi's stupa here. I said of course, that would be a great honor for us, and a fine way of saying farewell. We worked hard for several days, raking all the paths with devotion. Preparing the grounds for Rinpoche's arrival, we all felt we were working not merely to work, but to actualize a life of compassion and wisdom. That is true *samu*. One resident was assigned to clear weeds from the path leading to Suzuki-roshi's stupa. He was obviously trying too hard; he had found a big mower, and with it cut too much. The moment I saw how bare the pathway looked, how lacking in intimacy, I felt upset with him. Then I remembered that Rinpoche was lame and needed help walking, and realized that probably this eager student had done just the right thing! Beyond the path, where we'd cleaned the grounds beautifully, I felt we had cleaned our minds too. How important it is to remember that when you clean anything, you are essentially cleaning yourself. You assume you're just raking weeds and pebbles, but you're actually raking clean your mind.

When it turned out that Rinpoche was ill and couldn't come, we were disappointed. But soon, down that long path to Suzuki-roshi's stupa, dozens of bright red flowers bloomed! This was the only year that had ever happened. It was as though Trungpa Rinpoche had arrived in another form! Of course, such phenomena are perfectly natural, and even ordinary, in the Buddhadharma. Still, they are remarkable and auspicious occurrences.

POSTSCRIPT: THE STORY OF CHÖGYAM TRUNGPA'S STUPA AT GENJO-JI

We are probably the only Zen community in North America with a stupa to Chögyam Trungpa Rinpoche. If I am your Zen teacher, and we practice in the Zen tradition, then why do I invite this Shambhala sangha here? Why do we have a stupa for Trungpa Rinpoche, here on this land? Why was it built here?

Chögyam Trungpa entered *parinirvana* at Karmê Chöling on April 4, 1987, and the vajra regent of the Shambhala community presented us with Rinpoche's relics the following spring. It was clear then that we should build a stupa in his honor. So we proceeded to clear a wooded area in line with Suzuki-roshi's stupa, and built the stupa for Chögyam Trungpa Rinpoche. This was a testament to the deep friendship between these two remarkable teachers.

Many teachers of different traditions took part in the preparation. The Korean Zen Master Seung Sahn, an expert geomancer, chose the power spot on our mountain grounds. A Huichol Indian shaman from northern Mexico arrived to bless the spot. Wearing traditional, brightly colored, hand-embroidered clothing, he sat under the red banner, chanting.

Chagdud Rinpoche and his sangha joined us to purify the area late one night, as we watched the full moon appear over the mountain. The master thangka painter Noedup Rongae painted the appropriate images for the shrine. The master carpenter Paul Zengyu Discoe designed and built the stupa itself. Throughout this project, both sanghas gathered together on many weekends to work on the site. When the project was completed, we held a special ceremony honoring Trungpa Rinpoche. On October 28, 1990, hundreds of people arrived here for the *mahasangha* stupa ceremony.

That afternoon, as I read a poem I had written for the occasion, I realized that tears were streaming down my face. It wasn't that I simply missed Trungpa Rinpoche. It was deep gratitude for all the difficult and pleasant experiences that we had shared. Those precious moments continue to show me the way that past time becomes present.

Here is the poem that I wrote:

> Three and a half seasons have passed since your parinirvana
> Now the mahasangha is all standing
> In front of your *shari* Stupa.
> Because the true stupa is formless, it is hard to see
> Yet how could one not see it?
> A Chinese Chan master once said,
> "A clear pool does not admit the turquoise dragon's coils."
> What does this mean?
> *KATSU!**
> May we be forgiven for each stone moved
> And for things destroyed in the making of this stupa.
> May you, Trungpa Rinpoche, consider this spot
> On Sonoma Mountain your dwelling place.
> May the spirit of this one taste
> Permeate the world.

*This is a Zen shout.—Ed.

DYING WELL

*Forget your small self, confined by conceptual thinking
to a box from which escape is difficult. In Zen,
we say that you are the box.*

YOU KNOW, all those things you want to deny—emptiness, loss, and death—are essential parts of life. You'll encounter them all one day, but it's better to face these obstacles sooner rather than later, so you can befriend them. Don't wait until you're dying to investigate your spiritual nature. You need to look at life as it comes, moment by moment. Don't waste time! If you begin to practice zazen meditation now, you'll unearth your intrinsic *prajna*. With *prajna*, you'll find a deep well of compassion you didn't realize you had, and you can truly help others as well as yourself. As you develop this more relaxed, open state of being through zazen practice, you'll find it an infallible means of dying well, without fear, regret, or rage.

The true practice of dying well is to see your life unfolding as a dream, so that you forget your small self, confined by conceptual thinking to a box from which escape is difficult. In Zen, we say that you *are* the box. Once you realize that, then you're actually *out* of the box. In reality, there's actually no problem in the box itself. Everyone is frantically trying to escape, but what about simply being in it? If you can forget who you are, then you are liberated from your self, your ideas, conceptions, and projections. Even if you stay in the box, liberation is possible.

Sometimes you dream and long for things you cannot do. But when you are in *samadhi*, liberated from your deluded thoughts, there's no need to dream that way. Your life itself is the dream unfolding; it's beyond your likes and dislikes, beyond what you think you must protect yourself from. Understanding your life, viewing it in this relaxed, open state, you have an opportunity to learn how to die well.

In practicing meditation, you return to what you already have. You'll certainly die well if you come to recognize this intrinsic nature of yours, your buddha-nature, because you become peace itself. Seeing your life as a dream, a cloud, a bubble, you'll realize how to die while living.

Realization is sometimes referred to as a great death, but this means it's that old-habit part of you that has to die. You have to learn how to die while you are alive. Don't wait until you're dying. Just how do you learn how to die while you're living? Give up. You know when you're clinging to something? Just let it go. Don't hold on so tight. There is always impermanence and uncertainty in our lives, even as we're trying to make things secure and solid. And the biggest uncertainty is death. No one knows when we will die. The wisdom of insecurity lies in accepting impermanence unconditionally.

In confronting dying or death, some of you here have come close. Actually, just being born brings you close to death, whether you know it or not. One of the essentials in meditation practice is an understanding of dying.

Suzuki-roshi once said, "We practice zazen like someone close to dying. There is nothing to rely on, nothing to depend on. Because you are dying, you don't want anything, so you cannot be fooled by anything."

The Buddha's "eternal life" involves knowing what death is, nonconceptually. You discover in your practice how to die over and over and over again, which is really the meaning of "eternal life." To die is to give yourself up in zazen; this, in a way, is a kind of rehearsal for your physical death. Your mental approach to death will influence your physical death, certainly. But it's also what will give you eternal life. There's practicality here, a relative to this absolute. That's why dying in zazen is a great benefit.

A little koan: two monks, Tao Wu and Chien Yuan, are making a condolence call.

Yuan hits the coffin and asks, "Is the person inside alive or dead?"

Wu replies, "I won't say if the person's alive. I won't say that the person's dead, either."

I think only Zen people could ask something like this! The average person doesn't really understand the meaning of "alive" and "dead," of birth-and-death. Because we think that we're born and then die, we're in the box. So, is the person inside the box alive or dead?*

---

*This koan is like the case of Schroedinger's cat.—Ed.

REMEMBERING
MITSU SUZUKI

MITSU SUZUKI, my teacher's wife, died in 2016 at the age of one hundred and one. Mrs. Suzuki was a truly accomplished person. Even in her old age she still had a vibrant, strong spirit, and she died a good death. She was a mentor to me, and a great friend.

I still remember when Mrs. Suzuki first came to America, sailing into San Francisco on a freighter. We students were on the pier with Suzuki-roshi, watching the ship come into the harbor. At the ship's railing was this tiny woman waving her hands and arms—really waving, you know, with her whole body. She *was* the wave. She had that kind of youthful liveliness.

At home in San Francisco, she welcomed many of us young Zen students into her kitchen, where she would offer her direct, friendly, and unassuming advice. Her activity was a beautiful example of Zen in daily life. And she had a great mischievous sense of humor. Sometimes a student would ask her if Suzuki-roshi was enlightened. At this, she would just kick her husband under the table and laugh.

In the early days at the Bush Street temple we had our formal *oryoki* meals in their kitchen. During *oryoki* breakfast Mitsu, having just woken up, would come right into the kitchen to brush her teeth, looking disheveled, her hair in a tangle. She would go to the sink, and, while we tried to maintain our silent focus, she'd brush her teeth and gargle loudly, as if we weren't there.

Years later, before evening zazen at San Francisco Zen Center on Page Street, Mrs. Suzuki would often invite me into her kitchen for a bite. One time when she was making noodles, she added a lot of hot wasabi, saying that this would make me give a good strong Dharma talk. She knew I was very shy in those days.

One evening when I was on my way to zazen, Mitsu said, "Let's go to a movie!" What a surprise—then I wouldn't have to sit zazen! So Katagiri and I both sneaked out of zazen to see a Japanese movie with her. It was a romance film in which the couple was separated during World War II, the husband going off to war. Mrs. Suzuki cried openly throughout the whole movie. I realized that this had happened to her during the war, when she was married to her first husband. He was a bombardier on flying missions over China and was finally shot down there. She used to write him letters, saying, "Don't drop the bomb on the Chinese, because they are people just like us." She still had his picture hanging up at home. Later, she asked me if I could find out where in China he had been shot down, so she could visit that place, but we never had an opportunity to look for it.

Right now, I am reminded of Mitsu Suzuki as I see the flowers on the altar—bright red azaleas. This red azalea was a favorite of Suzuki-roshi's. He died on the fourth of December, and December eighth is the Buddha's Enlightenment Day. So commemorating Suzuki-roshi's death at the same time as Rohatsu, Buddha's Enlightenment Day, is really a double celebration for us.

On the day of Suzuki-roshi's funeral at the San Francisco Zen Center, I was helping Mrs. Suzuki as she was arranging azaleas to be displayed on the altar. Just before she finished, she

Mitsu Suzuki and Jakusho Kwong on the Sangha House
porch, Sonoma Mountain Zen Center

sipped some water without swallowing it, and she sprayed it—
whhshhh!—on the azalea, by blowing the water out with her mouth! I
was a young student at the time, and her action left a deep impression
on me.

Now we have those spray bottles, and you just go like this—*spritz
spritz*—but there's no spirit. It's the bottle that's doing the work. You
yourself are not doing it anymore. This memory of Mrs. Suzuki is etched
in my mind and heart to this day. That was in 1971.

Suzuki-roshi asked Mitsu to do three things after he died: stay at San Francisco Zen Center for ten years, learn to write Zen haiku poetry, and master the practice of the tea ceremony. Those three things.

She stayed at San Francisco Zen Center for the next twenty years, studying haiku and continuing to be a vibrant presence in the sangha.

She became a recognized haiku poet, several times winning the Eihei-ji haiku poetry award. I think maybe it was haiku that made her live so long. An example of her haiku shows her love of the ordinary:

> I bow to my ballpoint pen
> and throw it out—
> year's end

Fulfilling her husband's third request, Mrs. Suzuki became an accomplished tea ceremony sensei. She was a tea master of the Omotesenke school.

Before she departed to return to Japan, after the many years at San Francisco Zen Center, Mitsu came up to Genjo-ji. She wanted to visit Suzuki-roshi's stupa here to say goodbye.

We walked down the path through the woods to the stupa area and, after offering incense and bows and ladling water over Suzuki-roshi's stone stupa, we left. On the path back Mitsu asked me to pick some of the wild iris that had begun to grow that very year. She instructed me to pick the ones that hadn't quite blossomed. She tied one bud with a long blade of grass as we walked out. Then, in the turnout, she gave a big shout—"GOODBYE!" I was really startled!

We went on to Mitsu's farewell party, bringing the wild iris bud. A group of students had gathered to perform the formal *omote* tea ceremony. I had no idea what it would be like, but it was three hours of hell! Hours passed and my legs hurt so badly that I began to squirm in my *seiza* position. This made me realize that the practice of tea is no other than Zen.

Jakusho Kwong and Mitsu Suzuki at Shunryu Suzuki's stupa,
Sonoma Mountain Zen Center

After all the students had performed the ritual, Mitsu's turn came
to make tea. Then seventy-eight years old, she slowly arose from *seiza*,
walked slowly and steadily across the tatami, again sat in *seiza* and began.
She was not performing. She became tea. She *was* tea. The room was
silent, filled with the spirit of tea. And at precisely the same moment she

Kwong-roshi visiting Mitsu Suzuki at her home in Japan

poured, the tied wild iris bud, now in a vase on the *tokanoma*, suddenly burst open—there was so much energy in the room! This sort of mysterious occurrence is not uncommon in our Dharma world.

During her visit at Sonoma Mountain Zen Center, Mitsu marveled at the clear night sky and remarked that this was the first time she had ever seen the Milky Way the whole time she lived in America.

Many years later, my son Nyoze and I visited Mitsu in Shizuoka, Japan, perhaps for the last time. As I was leaving her, she gripped my hand with such surprising strength that it left an indelible imprint in my mind. I immediately knew this was our last moment together.

At the age of one hundred and one, Mitsu Suzuki-sensei died a good death on January 9, 2016, having lived a very full life. I will never miss her; she is forever with me.

At her memorial service at San Francisco Zen Center, I read a farewell poem. After the service, I asked to receive her ashes so they could be placed with Suzuki-roshi's at his stupa here on Sonoma Mountain. As this was one of Mitsu's last wishes, I was very happy to have it fulfilled.

Mitsu Suzuki's book of one hundred haiku, *A White Tea Bowl*,* was published to celebrate her hundredth birthday. It contains the following poem:

> Birth and death
> not holding on to even one thing—
> autumn brightness

*Mitsu Suzuki, *A White Tea Bowl: 100 Haiku from 100 Years of Life*, ed. by Kazuaki Tanahashi, trans. by Kate McCandless (Boulder: Shambhala Publications, 2014).

SEKITO'S HERMITAGE

S EKITO KISEN (Ch. Shitou Xiqian), disciple of Eno, was the eighth-century Chinese Zen master who paved the way for our Soto Zen school.

His name translates as "Above the Rock—Rare Transformation," but he was nicknamed Stonehead. When he retired from the monastery he had founded, he built himself a grass hut nearby. He lived there in seclusion for the rest of his life, and would sit zazen outside on a large rock above the hermitage. He died in 790 CE at the age of ninety. Such historical figures come alive to this day; you can still visit that very place where he lived. It's a rocky area surrounded by a metal fence, with a single large stone, and behind it a small plateau. Carved on that stone are kanji for "ancestor" and "source." This is the physical location of our ancestral origin.

Perhaps Sekito Kisen is best known for the "Sandokai," a poem frequently chanted in Soto Zen services. "Sandokai: The Intimacy of Relative and Absolute" was meant to resolve a dispute over interpretation between two Zen schools, identified as the Northern School and the Southern School. The "Sandokai" continues to be significant today, as humanity continues to suffer from ignorance and dualistic thinking.

However, his other great poem, "Song of the Grass-Roof Hermitage," written toward the end of his life, is more deeply personal, and reflects his own *ango* retreat, which he called "peaceful dwelling."

The poem does not say whether it's about his hut or simply about Sekito himself. Which is which? Maybe they're interchangeable; maybe they're totally the same. What we do know is that inside the hut there's nothing of value.

Emphasizing the impermanence of his whole existence, Sekito describes how, as soon as the grass-roofed hut is completed, fresh weeds appear. Completion, like permanence, is an illusion. The hut has finally been built, but it's never completely finished. Everything is moving and changing, endlessly.

Completion is like being on a hundred-foot pole. We may think we've reached the top, but in fact the pole has no top; it goes up endlessly. In the same way, our practice—like the Dharma—is endless.

Sekito knows that even though the hut is inhabited, fresh weeds continually spring up, and he doesn't mind at all. There is no *but* in the line "The person in the hut lives here calmly."

He is neither exclusively inside nor outside, nor even in between. He lives in his hut in complete serenity, comfortable with impermanence, open to everything.

Just so in meditation practice, *samadhi* is neither in nor beyond nor between body and mind. Where is it then? Pay attention. Is your sitting practice inward and claustrophobic? Is it external? Is it somewhere in between? Or is it all-pervasive?

Sekito says he won't live in places where worldly people live. It isn't that he hasn't any compassion for worldly people, but he doesn't participate in their conditioning, their lives of delusion and habitual discrimination, saying, "Realms worldly people love he does not love." He is not attached to the things that ordinary people desire and treasure, like big houses or expensive clothes and jewelry, because they have no meaning. He has given all that up. For Sekito, his small hut includes the entire universe.

Remember E. F. Schumacher, writing in the early 1970s? He coined the phrase "small is beautiful." I wonder if he understood that what he called small is actually the universe, the profound beauty of the whole universe.

Though Sekito's grass hut is only ten feet square, it includes everything. In his ten feet, the number ten represents perfection. Ten is also analogous to the number of decades he lived. Ninety years is the age at which an old man becomes illuminated: he arrives at realization, and has no more dualistic doubt. Here Sekito implies that he has attained enlightenment and become a bodhisattva who "trusts without doubt." He knows the Dharma unconditionally, through and through.

Isn't that exactly what we're aiming for in our zazen practice? If we have thousands of thoughts, we need to go to their source, ask who's producing them, and then turn our light inward as they vanish. *Samadhi* and *prajna* are the antidote. When we're flooded by ideas and feelings, we needn't be overwhelmed by them, because we know their nature. We can actually feel appreciation for them, since we can see them as expressions of the one nature that is everything.

The hut may be seen as Sekito himself, and fresh weeds appearing are the delusions that continue to arise.

"Perishable or not, the original master is present, not dwelling south or north, east or west." The original master—that is, the original self or buddha-nature—is always present. Buddha-nature does not dwell in any particular place. It is with us everywhere, if only we realize it.

If Sekito doesn't seem to understand anything at all, people won't take advantage of him; they'll think he's useless, a fool. In Zen, being useless, or not understanding, really means wisdom—*only don't know*. So Sekito lives without discriminating. He won't "proudly arrange seats trying to entice guests." He has no need to engage in society, or to speak to anyone at all.

In Sekito's next lines, he advises us to "turn around the light to shine within" our selves until that light has its own steadiness, its own stability.

You can't grasp buddha-nature by looking at it directly; it is not some *thing*, not objective reality. At the same time, you can't avoid it; it's everywhere.

"The vast inconceivable source cannot be faced nor turned away from."

If you study the ancestors' Dharma teachings deeply, and practice wholeheartedly without giving up, you can "let go of hundreds of years and relax completely." Sekito is saying that you let go of all your karma—past, present, and future.

Sekito's question, "Who would properly arrange seats trying to entice guests?" also means "Why would you want to invite thoughts?" He says to turn around the light to shine within; when you shine within, you return to yourself.

What is your potential? Are you capable of receiving the Dharma? Sitting zazen is training, a discipline to reveal your true nature. You cultivate it through your own practice. Little by little, your practice will grow strong, and ultimately you will have unconditional confidence in the Dharma. Your capability will grow through the steadfastness of your practice. It's a matter of turning your radiance inward, over and over and over. Then you'll realize your no-nature, which is the nature of the whole universe, which is emptiness.

SONG OF
THE GRASS-ROOF
HERMITAGE

Song of the Grass-Roof Hermitage

I've built a grass hut where there's nothing of value.
After eating, I relax and enjoy a nap.
When the hut was completed, fresh weeds appeared.
Now it's been lived in—covered by weeds.

The person in the hut lives here calmly,
Not stuck to inside, outside, or in-between.
Places worldly people live, he doesn't live.
Realms worldly people love, she doesn't love.

Though the hut is small, it includes the entire world.
In ten feet square, an old man illumines forms and their nature.
A Mahayana bodhisattva trusts without doubt.
The middling or lowly can't help wondering;
Will this hut perish or not?

Perishable or not, the original master is present,
not dwelling south or north, east or west.
Firmly based on steadiness, it can't be surpassed.
A shining window below the green pines—
jade palaces or vermilion towers can't compare with it.

Shitou Xiqian (700–790). Translated by Taigen Dan Leighton and Kazuaki Tana-hashi. From Taigen Dan Leighton, *Cultivating the Empty Field: The Silent Illumination of Zen Master Hongzhi* (Boston: Tuttle Publishing, 2000), 72–73.

Just sitting with head covered, all things are at rest.
Thus, this mountain monk doesn't understand at all.
Living here he no longer works to get free.
Who would proudly arrange seats, trying to entice guests?

Turn around the light to shine within, then just return.
The vast inconceivable source can't be faced or turned away from.
Meet the ancestral teachers, be familiar with their instruction,
bind grasses to build a hut, and don't give up.

Let go of hundreds of years and relax completely.
Open your hands and walk, innocent.
Thousands of words, myriad interpretations
are only to free you from obstructions.
If you want to know the undying person in the hut,
Don't separate from this skin bag here and now.

SONG of the GRASS ROOF HERMITAGE — SEKITO KISEN

I'VE BUILT a GRASS HUT
WHERE THERE IS NOTHING of VALUE.
AFTER EATING I RELAX & ENJOY a NAP.
WHEN IT WAS COMPLETED
FRESH WEEDS APPEARED.
NOW IT'S BEEN LIVED IN—
COVERED by WEEDS.
THE PERSON in the HUT
LIVES THERE CALMLY, NOT STUCK
to INSIDE, OUTSIDE, or in BETWEEN.
PLACES WORLDLY PEOPLE LIVE,
HE DOESN'T LIVE.
REALMS WORLDLY PEOPLE LOVE,
HE DOESN'T LOVE.
THOUGH the HUT is SMALL
IN INCLUDES the ENTIRE WORLD.
IN TEN SQUARE FEET, an OLD MAN
ILLUMINATES FORMS & NATURE.
A GREAT VEHICLE BODHISATTVA
TRUSTS WITHOUT DOUBT.
THE MIDDLING or LOWLY
CAN'T HELP WONDERING;
WILL THIS HUT PERISH or NOT?
PERISHABLE or NOT, the ORIGINAL
MASTER is PRESENT.

NOT DWELLING SOUTH or NORTH,
EAST or WEST,
FIRMLY BASED ON STEADINESS,
IT CAN'T BE SURPASSED.
A SHINING WINDOW
BELOW GREEN PINES —
JADE PALACES or VERMILION TOWERS
CAN'T COMPARE WITH IT.
JUST SITTING WITH HEAD COVERED
ALL THINGS ARE AT REST.
THUS, THIS MOUNTAIN MONK
DOESN'T UNDERSTAND AT ALL.
LIVING HERE HE NO LONGER
WORKS TO GET FREE
WHO WOULD PROUDLY ARRANGE SEATS,
TRYING TO ENTICE GUESTS?
TURN AROUND THE LIGHT TO SHINE
WITHIN, THEN JUST RETURN.
THE VAST INCONCEIVABLE SOURCE
CAN'T BE FACED & TURNED AWAY FROM.
MEET THE ANCESTRAL TEACHERS, BE
FAMILIAR WITH THEIR INSTRUCTIONS,
BIND GRASSES to BUILD a HUT, &
DON'T GIVE UP
LET GO of ONE HUNDREDS of
YEARS & RELAX COMPLETELY.

OPEN YOUR HANDS & WALK,
INNOCENT.
THOUSANDS of WORDS,
MYRIAD INTERPRETATIONS,
ARE ONLY to FREE YOU from OBSTRUCTIONS.
IF YOU WANT to KNOW the UNDYING
PERSON in the HUT,
DO NOT SEPARATE from THIS
SKIN BAG HERE & NOW.

THE GREAT FIRE
ON SONOMA MOUNTAIN

*Kwong-roshi wrote this letter to the sangha following the huge
firestorm in Northern California in 2017.*

I WANTED TO SHARE WITH YOU my experience of this great fire,
which came here on October 8, 2017. Under the mandatory evacuation
order, we fled at 2:00 AM on Monday, October 10. We grabbed a few
things and my son Nyoze drove Shinko and me out. The fire was burning right up to the road that we were driving on. We could hear propane
tanks exploding repeatedly—it sounded just like war; it *was* war. But
with good karma, we were all safe. Now we were refugees.

We stayed at Cam and Karen's place in Marin County for a week,
and then at my sister Emily's in Palo Alto. Nyoze left the second day,
returning to Sonoma Mountain to fight the fires. Staying at Em's house
was an interesting experience because there never would have been a
reason to be with her otherwise. The fire brought us together—Emily
and Shinko, Julie, Ejo, and myself. Nyoze's wife, Julie, was the fire hotline
center at Emily's. There were Buddhist groups all over the world pray-
ing for us—from Samye Ling in Scotland, Zen centers in Poland and

Iceland, Tassajara, Kwan Um temples in Korea, even Tenzin Palmo's nunnery in Ladakh, and elsewhere.

Nyoze quickly returned to Genjo-ji alone. The rest of my family and I returned to Genjo-ji about two weeks later.

Nyoze made the difficult journey through the police barricades and ravine fires to join the few remaining residents, who had staunchly refused to be evacuated and remained to defend the Zen Center. As he was running up the mountain Nyoze realized that he could die in the fires, but he reached the Zen Center safely. Later, he ran down the trail through the woods to the memorial stupas. Offering bows in front of Chögyam Trungpa's stupa, he climbed right up on the altar and seized the priceless thangka that Tibetan thangka painter Noedup Rongae had made for this stupa. The framed thangka was so heavy that Nyoze had to carry it on his back all the way back uphill, returning to the sangha house.

The residents were joined by other sangha members, and worked day and night in shifts—hosing down rooftops, putting out spot and smoldering fires with shovels, rakes, and hand-carried water, and using chainsaws to take down branches of trees that were on fire. The firestorm burned up Sonoma Mountain, stopping right beneath the foot of Suzuki-roshi's stupa! It stopped at the edge of Trungpa Rinpoche's stupa as well.

When the fire was approaching the Zen Center from the forest behind the stupas, the Bennett Valley fire department sent scouts and a bulldozer. The bulldozer dug a ten-foot wide trench as a fire break all the way from the neighboring property behind the stupas down toward Warm Springs Road. Approximately one third of the Zen Center's property was burned. The fire reached the bulldozed fire break right beneath the foot of Shunryu Suzuki-roshi's stupa.

The fire stopped right at the trench. The trench was what saved Suzuki-roshi's stupa, along with the entire Zen Center. In another area further up the path, the fire also stopped right at the grass around Trungpa's stupa, demonstrating the power of this place on Sonoma Mountain, and particularly the power of the stupas.

One crew of firefighters in Cooper's Grove, down where you drive through the redwoods on Sonoma Mountain Road, was a joint effort of first responders, firefighters, and neighbors—including even the nearby neighbor who was opposed to our Mandala Project building permit. It's interesting how *like* and *don't-like* all come together.

Responding to the fire brought people closer, melting boundaries and burning down fences that separate us. The fire made us come together to save each other, knowing that we were all in a great danger that would take not only our land and possessions, but our very lives.

Fire is like Manjushri's double-edged sword. One side of the blade takes or destroys life, while the other gives life. Fire joins people together by destroying and purifying the boundaries separating us. Fire clears open spaces for new growth and nourishment.

I personally am very grateful for all the first responders, for the thoughts and prayers from all over the world, and especially for our Zen fire warriors, who had the courage and fierceness to stay, saving Sonoma Mountain's Zen temple. It is HERE! We sit zazen, and we stand ever so tall, to uphold a rare and calm space open for everyone's return.

Our hearts are with all the victims, homes, trees, vegetation, animals, and insects that were less fortunate.

To give closure to this disaster, we held two ceremonies for our members and neighbors. Each ceremony was well attended, emotional, and full of gratitude. As these were the first get-togethers of the Sonoma Mountain community, these were one of the fortunate outcomes of the great fire.

Appendixes

AN EXAMINATION of the TWELVE LINKS of EXISTENCE

1 ENVELOPED in the DARK of IGNORANCE,
BEINGS PREFORM THREE KINDS of ACTION
THAT THEIR EXISTENCE MIGHT CONTINUE,
PROCEEDING by SUCH ACTIONS to THEIR DESTINY.

2 CONDITIONED by SUCH ACTIONS,
CONSCIOUSNESS ARISES in the VARIOUS WORLDS.
WHEN CONSCIOUSNESS HAS THUS MIGRATED,
NAME-and-FORM OCCUR.

3 WHEN NAME-and-FORM OCCUR,
THE SIX SENSES ARISE.
ON the BASIS of SIX SENSES,
GENUINE CONTACT THEN ARISES.

4 THIS is ONLY BORN DEPENDENT
ON the EYE, ON FORM, and ON ATTENTION.
DEPENDENT UPON NAME-and-FORM
(VISUAL) CONSCIOUSNESS OCCURS.

5 THE GATHERING of THESE THREE
(OF EYE and FORM and CONSCIOUSNESS)
IS CONTACT; and FROM CONTACT,
FEELING COMES to PASS.

6 THROUGH the CIRCUMSTANCE of FEELING,
CRAVING COMES — CRAVING for a FEELING.
WHEN CRAVING HAS ARISEN, THERE is GRASPING
— AND of THIS THERE ARE FOUR KINDS.

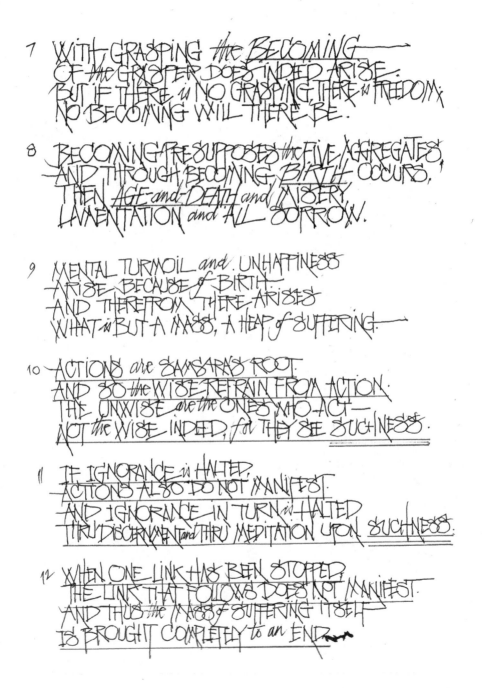

7 WITH GRASPING the BECOMING
OF the GRASPER DOES INDEED ARISE.
BUT IF THERE is NO GRASPING, THERE is FREEDOM:
NO BECOMING WILL THERE BE.

8 BECOMING PRE-SUPPOSES the FIVE AGGREGATES,
AND THROUGH BECOMING, BIRTH OCCURS,
THEN AGE-and-DEATH and MISERY
LAMENTATION and ALL SORROW.

9 MENTAL TURMOIL and UNHAPPINESS
ARISE BECAUSE of BIRTH.
AND THEREFROM THERE ARISES
WHAT is BUT A MASS, A HEAP of SUFFERING.

10 ACTIONS are SAMSARA'S ROOT.
AND SO the WISE REFRAIN FROM ACTION.
THE UNWISE are the ONES WHO ACT—
NOT the WISE INDEED, for THEY SEE SUCHNESS.

11 IF IGNORANCE is HALTED,
ACTIONS ALSO DO NOT MANIFEST.
AND IGNORANCE IN TURN is HALTED
THRU DISCERNMENT and THRU MEDITATION UPON SUCHNESS.

12 WHEN ONE LINK HAS BEEN STOPPED
THE LINK THAT FOLLOWS DOES NOT MANIFEST.
AND THUS the MASS of SUFFERING ITSELF
IS BROUGHT COMPLETELY to an END.

UNSHU INSTRUCTION

The following is a letter that Kwong-roshi wrote to one of his students.

INHALE BY BREATHING DEEPLY into the lower back through the kidneys until the diaphragm naturally becomes full. At just this point rest the mind in the palm of your left hand, within the cosmic mudra. Following this, exhale. Pause slightly at the end of exhalation before breathing in again.

This is the *unshu*. Focus on the natural sound of the breath. As you are breathing it, it also breathes you. When this process is repeated over and over, the rhythm of the breath gradually rises to a crescendo, doubling in strength. The natural strength of the *unshu* sound—*uuuuun*—dissolves any idea or thought of greed, anger, and ignorance. And you know what? Your buddha-nature is revealed! It is as simple as that.

Exhale from the *tanden*—the field of energy two inches below the navel—as well as from the nose. The exhalation goes from coarse to fine, released in a very fine stream. As soon as it seems to end, merge it into space. Chögyam Trungpa Rinpoche and Shunryu Suzuki-roshi both emphasized this point: you are returning home. You are returning home in your zazen practice. As sitting is repeated over and over again it confirms the confidence, wisdom, and compassion that you innately possess, so that you are prepared for almost anything.

Inhalation is spontaneous because you need air to live. The following instruction is less detailed: Inhale through the same places, drawing the air into the nose as well as the *tanden*, or from the back, in any creative combination that works for you. There's no need to listen for sound. When the diaphragm is full, pause slightly and then exhale—with the long *unshu* sound as above.

Naturally you should be aware that long or short breathing is only a condition. Here, long is just long and short is just short. When you begin to focus on your breath, most likely it will be short, but as you continue the sequence your exhalation will naturally become longer. The emphasis is on exhalation—the inhalation takes care of itself. This *unshu* sound—*uuuuun*—is not necessarily loud. It is natural and universal.

Basically, this is to remind you of what you are doing every day of your life. You already have this ability. *Unshu* exhalation transpires spontaneously in every action you execute and engage in. Just be aware and witness it for yourself—throwing a ball, swinging an axe, turning a door handle, going to the toilet, using the computer, and so on.

As long as you are free of physical restrictions, you can return home anywhere, at any time, because your breath is with you all your life. When you die, the exhalation is your last breath.

I think this covers it. After really practicing this for a while—and not just when you are sitting zazen—please send me a note and tell me what effect *unshu* has in your everyday life.

CREDITS

Excerpts from *Cultivating the Empty Field* by Taigen Dan Leighton with Yi Wu. Reprinted with permission from Tuttle Publishing.

Excerpts from *The Root Stanzas of the Middle Way: The Mulamadhyamakakarika* by Nagarjuna, translated by the Padmakara Translation Group. Copyright © 2008 by Editions Padmakara. Reprinted by arrangement with The Permissions Company, LLC, on behalf of Shambhala Publications Inc., Boulder, CO, shambhala.com.

Excerpts from *A White Tea Bowl: 100 Haiku from 100 Years of Life* by Mitsu Suzuki, translated by Kate McCandless. Copyright © 2014 by San Francisco Zen Center. Reprinted by arrangement with The Permissions Company, LLC, on behalf of Roost Books, an imprint of Shambhala Publications Inc., Boulder, CO, shambhala.com.

All photos are reprinted courtesy of the Sonoma Mountain Zen Center archives.

ABOUT THE AUTHOR

JAKUSHO KWONG was born in Santa Rosa, California, in 1935, and grew up in Palo Alto. As a boy he worked all summers with his mother in commercial flower growers' fields nearby. During and after his education he was employed in commercial art as a sign painter, and was drawn to calligraphy, particularly *zenga*, the art of Zen calligraphy.

In 1960 he began to study Zen with Shunryu Suzuki-roshi in San Francisco. He was ordained in 1970 by Suzuki-roshi, who was a direct spiritual descendant of Eihei Dogen. In 1973, two years after Suzuki-roshi died, he founded Sonoma Mountain Zen Center in the mountains near Santa Rosa, California, as an expression of gratitude to his teacher and his commitment to continue the unbroken lineage of Soto Zen. Since his study of the transmission ceremony could not be completed before Suzuki-roshi's death, he continued for five more years with Kobun Chino Otogawa-roshi. In 1978 he completed Dharma transmission through Hoitsu Suzuki-roshi under the supervision of Hakusan Noiri-roshi, at Rinso-in temple in Japan, authorizing him as a successor in Suzuki-roshi's lineage.

In 2009, he was appointed Kokusaifukyoshi (International Zen Teacher) of North America by the Soto School of Japan, which recognizes Sonoma Mountain Zen Center as an authentic Soto Zen temple.

Jakusho Kwong has taught Zen for more than fifty years, and founded Zen centers in Poland and Iceland. His first book, *No Beginning, No End*, was published in 2003.

He is abbot of Sonoma Mountain Zen Center, where he lives with his wife, Shinko.

WHAT TO READ NEXT
FROM WISDOM PUBLICATIONS

Being-Time
A Practitioner's Guide to Dogen's Shobogenzo Uji
Shinshu Roberts

"This book is a great achievement. Articulate, nuanced, and wonderful."
—Jan Chozen Bays, author of *Mindfulness on the Go*

Master Ma's Ordinary Mind
The Sayings of Zen Master Mazu Daoyi
Fumio Yamada
Translated by John Bellando

In *Master Ma's Ordinary Mind*, you will learn the true nature of enlightenment from one of Zen's great teachers. Master Mazu's teachings help us to see how our own "ordinary mind," just as it is, also functions as the mind of enlightenment—the very expression of buddhanature.

Inside the Grass Hut
Living Shitou's Classic Poem
Ben Connelly

Shitou Xiqian's "Song of the Grass Roof Hermitage" is a remarkably accessible work of profound depth; in thirty-two lines Shitou expresses the breadth of the entire Buddhist tradition with simple, vivid imagery. *Inside the Grass Hut* unpacks the timeless poem and applies it to contemporary life.

The Complete Illustrated Guide to Zen
Seigaku Amato

"This is a cute book! But it's not just cute, it's also deep and profound, and is one of the best guides to Zen practice I have ever come across. The illustrations are delightful and the written sections are clear and easy to understand. I give it a million zillion stars!"
—Brad Warner, author of *Hardcore Zen*

The Illustrated Lotus Sutra
Translation and introduction by Gene Reeves
Illustrations by Demi

This illustrated edition features more than 110 full-page and two-page illustrations by a world-renowned and award-winning artist, and brings the fantastical and image-filled world of the *Lotus Sutra* vividly to life.

The following spread shows an example of Shunryu Suzuki-roshi's calligraphy, which was part of his Dharma transmission to Jakusho Kwong-roshi. The margins contain notes on how to write the Chinese characters, or *kanji*. The words in all capitals indicate the pronunciation of each character, while the numerals indicate the order in which to draw each stroke. Japanese kanji is read vertically, from top to bottom and from right to left.

俊

RYU

MA

SO

TATSU

菩 BO.

温

薩 SATSU
4
3
2
1
2
3
4

禪

佛 BUTSU
1 7
6
3
4 2
5
0

心 SHIN
3 1
2
1 4

About Wisdom Publications

Wisdom Publications is the leading publisher of classic and contemporary Buddhist books and practical works on mindfulness. To learn more about us or to explore our other books, please visit our website at wisdomexperience.org or contact us at the address below.

Wisdom Publications
199 Elm Street
Somerville, MA 02144 USA

We are a 501(c)(3) organization, and donations in support of our mission are tax deductible.

Wisdom Publications is affiliated with the Foundation for the Preservation of the Mahayana Tradition (FPMT).